The Power of Myth

THE POWER OF MYTH

Israeli Propaganda and Christian Zionism

By
David M. Crump

Foreword by Brian Zahnd

CASCADE *Books* • Eugene, Oregon

THE POWER OF MYTH
Israeli Propaganda and Christian Zionism

Cascade Books
An Imprint of Wipf and Stock Publishers
199 W. 8th Ave., Suite 3
Eugene, OR 97401

www.wipfandstock.com

PAPERBACK ISBN: 979-8-3852-4305-1
HARDCOVER ISBN: 979-8-3852-4306-8
EBOOK ISBN: 979-8-3852-4307-5

Cataloguing-in-Publication data:

Names: Crump, David M., author. | Zahnd, Brian, foreword.

Title: The power of myth : Israeli propaganda and Christian Zionism / David M. Crump; foreword by Brian Zahnd.

Description: Eugene, OR: Cascade Books, 2026 | Includes bibliographical references and index.

Identifiers: ISBN 979-8-3852-4305-1 (paperback) | ISBN 979-8-3852-4306-8 (hardcover) | ISBN 979-8-3852-4307-5 (ebook)

Subjects: LCSH: Arab-Israeli conflict. | Bible—Geography. | Land tenure—Biblical teaching. | Land tenure—Middle East.

Classification: BS680.L25 C35 2026 (paperback) | BS680.L25 (ebook)

VERSION NUMBER 042126

Contents

Foreword

THEOLOGY IS NOT AN arcane activity reserved for a cadre of specialists—theology is simply how we think and what we say about God. To form an idea about the divine and to express that idea is to engage in theology. But Christian theology is not a domain where egalitarianism is privileged—not all ideas about the God revealed in Christ are equally valid. For example, seventeen centuries ago at the Council of Nicaea the Christian bishops settled a christological debate, confessing that Jesus is "true God from true God" and not a lesser being as Arius had taught. All of this matters because theology has real life consequences. And this is never more evident than when we bring our theology to the current Israeli–Palestinian conflict.

Christian Zionism is a prime and tragic example of how much harm can be done in the name of bad theology. I say this as one who in my youth inherited Christian Zionism as the default position within American evangelicalism. Some of this bad theology was received in good faith as an attempt to atone for the long, sad history of antisemitism in the church. But well-intended as it may be, Christian Zionism has a fatal flaw: It is not true to the New Testament.

Central to New Testament thought is the revelation that the covenant promises of God made to Abraham and David are fulfilled in Jesus Christ. We are alerted to this in the very first verse of the New Testament: "The genealogy of Jesus the Messiah, the son of David, the son of Abraham" (Matt 1:1). Jesus is the true seed of Abraham who blesses all the families of the earth and the true son of David who reigns forever. On the Emmaus Road the crucified and risen Christ showed his two traveling companions how the things written in Moses and the prophets were fulfilled by himself, and thus "he opened their minds to understand the scriptures" (Luke 24:45). In speaking of Christ, Paul says "in him every one of God's promises is a 'Yes'" (2 Cor 1:20). It is no exaggeration to state that the first

Jewish Christians saw the Old Testament as *all about Jesus*. But Christian Zionism seeks to subvert the high Christology of the New Testament by making the modern nation-state of Israel a kind of strange co-redemptrix with Christ—that somehow the promises of God are fulfilled by Jesus *and* by the modern nation-state of Israel. This leads to the theological error of giving to a political state the kind of unquestioned allegiance that belongs solely to Jesus Christ as Lord. Christian Zionism creates divided loyalties with catastrophic consequences.

Upon further scrutiny and as it plays out in real life, Christian Zionism is little more than substituting scapegoats—instead of Jews as their scapegoats, Christians will now scapegoat Palestinians. But scapegoating (achieving unity by projecting blame upon a vilified other) is not the way of the Christ; it is literally the way of the satan—the accuser. To advocate for the violent subjugation and forced removal of a people from their historic homeland though an aberrant reading of select Old Testament texts is utterly contrary to the way of love and mercy taught by Jesus. David Crump puts it bluntly when he writes, "Christ never approves of mass slaughter, oppression, discrimination, or stripping people of their dignity." That such a self-evident sentence should *need* to be written shows how dangerous Christian Zionism has become.

One of its most intractable problems is that Christian Zionism refuses to read the New Testament in a theologically serious manner. This is especially true in regard to the Pauline epistles. Paul's grand theological project was to offer a solution to the first big controversy the church faced: How do you justify gentiles *as* gentiles being full members of the Jewish body of Messiah? Through a creative and inspired re-reading of the Old Testament, Paul reveals that in Messiah's death the dividing wall between Jews and gentiles has been broken down, "that he might create in himself one new humanity" (Eph 2:15). Participation in the covenant of God is no longer defined by ethnicity, circumcision, and Torah observance, but by faith, baptism, and obedience to Jesus. In the historic person of a particular Galilean Jew, the salvation of God is made universally accessible. In Christ the chosen people are now the human race, and the holy land is now the whole earth. This may seem to be a radical reinterpretation of the Old Testament (though it was really there all along), but it is clearly the inspired apostolic interpretation of the New Testament.

Christian Zionism, on the other hand, is an assault upon the high Christology of the New Testament and Paul's theology of justification.

Thus, while it may be Zionism, it is hardly Christian—at least not in any credibly theological way. A faithful reading of the New Testament must not be jettisoned in favor of political agendas and pop eschatology. The apostle Paul is not subject to the partisan politics of John Hagee or the macabre fiction of Tim LaHaye.

My utter rejection of Christian Zionism as incompatible with sound Christian theology does not mean that I don't love Israel and the Jewish people. I do. But I also love Palestine and the Palestinian people—especially my Palestinian brothers and sisters in Christ. None of this is abstract to me. I've been to Israel and Palestine dozens of times. I suppose I've lived a year of my life in that land. I've been in the West Bank. I've been in Gaza—which is something very few Israelis have done . . . unless they were toting a gun. When you stop thinking of people in abstraction and meet them face to face, or better yet, over a shared meal, a lot can change. I know it has changed me, and I've seen this kind of human interaction change others as well.

Ultimately Christian Zionism comes to an end when we learn to the read the Bible in the light of Christ—the way the first Christians read the Bible. It's not Joshua and his wars of conquest that inform Christian theology, but Jesus Christ and him crucified. It's not Saul's genocidal slaughter of Amalekite men, women, children, and babies that informs Christian ethics, but the Sermon on the Mount. It's not David's wars with the Philistines that informs Christian eschatology, but the Lamb's self-sacrificial conquest of the principalities and powers. The purposes of God are *entirely* fulfilled in the crucified and risen Christ. That simple but incontrovertible statement alone renders Christian Zionism theologically incoherent.

And now a book awaits you. A book that is powerful and provocative, but a book that is also theologically robust and deeply Christian. It's not reckless but well-researched. This book is not hypothetical or serene; it is timely and urgent. It is a book that proceeds from real passion and a profound desire to follow Jesus. Near the very end of this significant work, David Crump writes, "My goal is not to change pro-Israel people into pro-Palestinian people. My objective, rather, is to help us all become pro-humanity people." And in light of the apostle Paul telling us that the accomplishment of Christ upon the cross was to form one new humanity in himself, to become a person who is pro-humanity really is the apex of Christian discipleship.

Brian Zahnd, author of *The Wood Between the Worlds*

Acknowledgments

WRITING TENDS TO BE a solitary pursuit. Good editing, on the other hand, requires friends. The production of *The Power of Myth: Israeli Propaganda & Christian Zionism* has been no exception.

My editorial process has been markedly improved by the contributions of three friends. Michael Thomson, a member of the editorial staff at Wipf & Stock, was diligent in providing helpful editorial advice throughout the writing process.

Gary Burge kindly offered insightful suggestions for improvement chapter by chapter.

Rob Dalrymple also provided helpful encouragement about the finished manuscript at the final stage of its composition.

Many thanks are due to these good friends.

As always, any mistakes or errors in judgment remain mine alone. I don't always take my editors' advice.

INTRODUCTION
Zionist Mythology, Israeli Propaganda, and Christian Zionism

October 7, 2023, has entered the annals of history, signifying inhumane atrocities committed against the Jewish citizens of Israel by Gazan militants. It's a date and an event to be remembered in the same way that September 11, 2001, and the destruction of the Twin Towers are remembered in the United States.

Beginning at 6:30 a.m. on that day hundreds of armed Palestinian militants began to penetrate the military barriers that separated the Gaza Strip from the numerous communities built in proximity to the Gaza separation wall. Moving quickly in cars, on motorcycles, and motorized hang gliders, members of Hamas and Palestinian Islamic Jihad attacked these Jewish communities with automatic weapons and rocket propelled grenades. Before the day was over approximately twelve hundred people, men, women, and children, would be killed and left where they fell. Two hundred fifty-one people of all ages were taken back into Gaza as hostages. The horrors of that day have been told, retold, and memorialized by the Jewish community many times since then. And rightly so.

October 7 and 9/11 are dates that live in infamy, and in Israel and the United States the fallen will continue to be mourned and memorialized. It should be understandable, then, when other people face their own similar horrors that such events burn themselves into their collective memories too. Let me list another series of recent dates that do just that, this time for the Palestinians. I wager that none of them, for my Western readers at least, will trigger the reflexive recall created by either October 7 or 9/11. Each of these events occurred in Israel and Gaza: May 2023, August 2022, May

2021, November 2021, July–August 2014, December 2008–January 2009. To begin, notice that these dates mark repeated traumas that occurred for more than a single day; all these dates mark an Israeli military operation against the people of Gaza, operations the IDF (Israel Defense Forces) commonly referred to as "mowing the grass" (or mowing the lawn).[1] As the potential for Palestinian armed resistance to a brutal Israeli occupation may increase over time, the Israeli military planned periodic, massive assaults against Gaza in order to weaken militant groups and to diminish their abilities to strike out at Israel. Each Israeli assault varied with any number of targets in the crosshairs. Yes, Israeli messaging would consistently describe each attack as another defensive action taken in response to Hamas missile fire. The public accounts of Israeli incursions all describe inevitable actions meant to protect Jewish Israelis from real or perceived threats. Perhaps no one could foretell the date of the next Gaza grass-mowing operation, but it would come as unavoidably as the rising of the morning sun.[2]

Let me associate some important names and numbers with these dates:[3] May 2023, Operation Shield and Arrow, 30 Palestinians killed (including four children); August 2022, Operation Breaking Dawn, 33 Palestinians killed (including nine children and three women); May 2021, Operation Guardian of the Walls, 233 Palestinians killed (54 children and 38 women); November 2021, Operation Pillar of Defense, 167 Palestinians killed (33 children and 13 women); July–August 2014, Operation Protective Edge, 2,188 Palestinians killed (548 children, 247 women); December 2008–January 2009, Operation Cast Lead, 1,417 Palestinians killed (313 children and 115 women).

All together the Israeli military killed at least 4,068 Palestinians in Gaza between December 2008 and May 2023. Operation Protective Edge alone killed twice as many people in Gaza as were killed in Israel on October 7. Operation Cast Lead killed several hundred more people in Gaza than were killed by Palestinians on October 7. My purpose is not simply to compare body counts, dead Palestinians versus Israeli Jews, although that is a necessary part of my analysis as well. My purpose is to highlight the fact that the horrible events that occurred on October 7, 2023, compose only

1. See Taylor, "With Strikes," for one discussion of this military practice.

2. Finkelstein, *Method and Madness*, and Shlaim, "Ten Years," both discuss the ways in which Israel precipitates these attacks while publicly justifying their assaults as self-defense.

3. Information gathered at B'Tselem, "Rounds of Fighting in Gaza."

one mark on a bloody timeline that features numerous repugnant events and thousands upon thousands of human deaths that go unnoticed and generally remain unmentioned because they involve the wrong sort of victims, unworthy victims generally ignored by Western media.[4] Throughout this book we will see how powerfully Israeli propaganda works to control these narratives. Palestinians suffer not only from a lack of PR, but from concerted efforts at disinformation that can make them all but invisible.

The effects of Israeli propaganda are everywhere evident in how we perceive Israelis and Palestinians who have been killed. For most Westerners there is a strong tendency to feel greater sympathy for the Jewish-Israeli victims of Palestinian aggression than we might feel for the Palestinian victims of Jewish-Israeli aggression. "Well, the twelve hundred victims on October 7 were all massacred on a single day; it wasn't spread out over a series of weeks. That makes it a greater tragedy," some may be thinking. But Operation Protective Edge saw an average of forty-four Palestinians killed by the IDF every day for fifty consecutive days in 2014. Isn't that equally horrific? What makes for the more egregious slaughter? Volume? Rapidity? The type of victims? The manner of their deaths? My purpose in asking these questions is not in any way to diminish the horrors of October 7 but to remind my readers that these events did not happen in a vacuum. And also to remind ourselves that all human life is equally valuable to God. All human beings are created as God's own image, as the *imago Dei*. But all deaths are not lamented equally by the public. This is not an accident in the case of Palestine, and I hope the following pages will provide a deeper ability to mourn the victims of Israeli violence just as we rightly mourn the Israelis who fell on October 7.

We tend to empathize most with those for whom we feel the greatest affinity. To a large extent, whatever affinity we feel for distant strangers caught up in a tragedy on foreign soil is curated for us by the way the media "frames" and tells the stories we read and watch on our phones, computers, and televisions. The specific ways in which journalists package a story, that is the way the story is told, what is emphasized, what is omitted, what details are highlighted up front, and which elements are buried till the end,

4. For the ways in which propaganda creates the distinction between worthy vs. unworthy victims, see Herman and Chomsky, *Manufacturing Consent*, 37–86; for a moving analysis of what it means for Palestinians at large to be seen as unworthy victims, see el-Kurd, *Perfect Victims*.

all this will have a powerful effect on what we believe we "know" about an event.[5]

When it comes to stories about Israel–Palestine, a close look at Western media of all sorts reveals a strong racist undercurrent in how these stories are told, which in turn shapes the ways white Americans respond to events in the Middle East. White Ashkenazi Jews descended from immigrants who moved to Israel from Eastern or Central Europe cut a more sympathetic figure to the average white American than do the brown-skinned Palestinian Arabs. In the news, as in most movies featuring Arabs in the West, the darker skinned Middle Easterners are habitually cast as the recalcitrant aggressor. Ironically, even when they are the ones being massacred by IDF missile strikes, Palestinians are typically presented as "deserving it" in some way or another for their perennial misbehavior. Israeli Jews are typically cast as the innocent victims who continue to suffer unjustly. Palestinians, on the other hand, remain the stubborn aggressors forever unwilling to live with Israel in peace. This Manichaean dichotomy—Israeli Jews good, Palestinian Arabs bad—suffuses the atmosphere of Western cultures, largely unnoticed but nonetheless real. Nearly fifty years ago the Palestinian American scholar of comparative literature Edward Said insightfully described this presumptive disparagement of Arab voices and labeled it "Orientalism." His words remain as relevant today as they were when he first wrote them:

> Orientalism governs Israeli policy towards the Arabs throughout. . . . There are good Arabs (the ones who do as they are told) and bad Arabs (who do not, and are therefore terrorists). Most of all there are all those Arabs who, once defeated, can be expected to sit obediently behind an infallibly fortified line, manned by the smallest possible number of men on the theory that Arabs have had to accept the myth of Israeli superiority and will never dare attack.[6]

Perhaps my reader's discomfort has slightly deepened at my suggestion that American loyalty to Israel and sympathy for Jewish suffering is more complicated than mere empathy for the little guy. Aside from the fact that Israel has never really been the "little guy" in its contest with the surrounding Arab states (see chapter 4), political Zionism—the animating strain of Zionism that lies at the heart of the modern nation-state of

5. For a discussion of framing as it specifically relates to news coverage of Israel–Palestine, see Shupak, *Wrong Story*.

6. Said, *Orientalism*, 306.

Israel—has always had several strains of racism at its core. Indeed, racism is an indelible part of the founding myth that makes Israeli Zionism what it is.

Zionist Mythology

Nations cannot exist without a founding mythology; such founding myths lay the basis of nationhood.[7] A nation without a mythology is like a child without parentage. For example, the founding myth of America began with the Puritan conviction that they were the new Israel displacing the Native American "Canaanites" as they carved a new Zion out of the dark, primordial forests hugging America's eastern seaboard. Eventually, that myth of civilized conquest overtaking a barren wilderness filled with wild savages was expanded as North American settlement moved into the middle prairies, the Rocky Mountains, and the high plains of the American West, always marching inexorably to the Pacific coast. It was a divine destiny that would eventually be called Manifest.

These founding, national mythologies serve at least five purposes in shaping the character and the mindset of a nation's citizenry.[8] First, founding myths tell the story of a people's collective origins; they tell us where we've come from and how we got to where we are today. Second, such myths also give us a sense of direction, pointing us to where we are going in the future and what our eventual destiny may look like if we remain true to our national calling. Third, national myths offer a sense of personal identity, answering the questions of who I am, and how I am situated within the cosmos, within this world, within my own national story. Fourth, mythologies provide the basis for community, a collective identity that connects me with "my tribe" and explains to me why we belong together. Finally, founding myths create a foundation for our basic moral values, our sense of right and wrong, shaping the kind of people we should want to be; they also tell us who our enemies are and who we must fight against if we hope to fulfill our destiny.

Israel's founding mythology fulfills all of these purposes including the national objectives of racial, ethnic exclusion. Not everyone can be included among the chosen people, after all. The indigenous peoples of North America were never intended to share in the white supremacist, colonial goals of

7. Strenski, *Four Theories*, 16, explaining the view of Ernst Cassirer.

8. See May, *Cry for Myth*, 15, 20, 30–31; Strenski, *Four Theories*, 72–73, expressing the views of Mircea Eliade.

Manifest Destiny. Their fate was one of exclusion, erasure, and isolation on reservations located on marginal lands passed over by the white man. In the same vein, the nation of Israel has always been a colonial ethnocracy, a racially defined,[9] Jewish supremacist state where all non-Jews, but especially all Palestinian Arabs, can be nothing more than second-class citizens,[10] if in fact they hold any sort of citizenship at all.[11] Israel officially codified this most fundamental aspect of its identity in 2018 when the Knesset[12] passed the Basic Law—Israel as the Nation State of the Jewish People.[13] This law established, as a part of Israel's effective constitution, that the land of Israel was the historic home of the Jewish people alone, giving Jews and *only Jews* the legal right to national self-determination. Consequently, the indigenous Palestinian people who have lived there for centuries have no rights to equal status under the law, nor can they collectively, publicly define or express their own national identity as ancient residents of Palestine.[14]

This modern, racist nation-state called Israel is the culmination of an endeavor first proposed in 1896 by Theodore Herzl in his little book titled *The Jewish State*, a foundational text for Zionist mythology. Herzl believed that the only possible cure for antisemitism was the creation of an all-Jewish state, a place where Jews could pursue their national development apart from gentiles. According to Herzl, Jews took antisemitism with them wherever they went since it erupted spontaneously whenever Jews mixed with non-Jews.[15] Leo Pinsker, a Zionist contemporary of Herzl's, similarly argued that antisemitism was an incurable, gentile psychosis.[16] The only solution was to keep the two peoples apart. The best way to succeed at such ethnic gerrymandering was the creation of a Jewish nation-state, a Jewish

9. Defining Jewishness as a racial rather than a religious term is an important Zionist innovation.

10. See Rouhana and Huneidi, *Israel and Its Palestinian Citizens*; Yiftachel, *Ethnocracy*.

11. Palestinian residents of Gaza and the West Bank are not allowed to hold Israeli citizenship.

12. The Knesset is Israel's parliament.

13. See Knesset, Basic Law.

14. Two Israeli human rights organizations are important in this regard: B'Tselem keeps track of the continuing violation of Palestinian human rights in the occupied territories, while Adalah catalogues the legal apparatus used to discriminate against Palestinians within Israel. Adalah lists sixty-five different Israeli laws that discriminate against Palestinian citizens.

15. Herzl, *Jewish State*, 50–53.

16. Herzl, *Jewish State*, 4.

ethnocracy, established on a "neutral piece of land" under "the protectorate" of a European colonial power.[17] This Jewish state would form "a rampart" for European culture, "an outpost of civilization" that would forever stand as a colonial bulwark against Middle Eastern barbarism.[18] Anticipating that the indigenous Arab peoples would eventually protest against a swelling tide of Jewish immigration, Herzl expected Zionism's colonial benefactor—Great Britain as it turned out to be—to contain Palestinian resistance while defending Zionism's "sovereign right" to continue its immigration program as enthusiastically as it pleased.[19]

We can see that Israel's origins were heavily salted with the matching poison pills of Orientalism mixed with European colonialism. Israel was established as a settler-colonial project. The racial prejudice and cultural hubris innate to such an imperial perspective on the world are essential ingredients to Zionist mythology. A very specific narrative unfolded which is perpetuated today:[20]

Jews have an eternal right to pursue their national self-determination in all the land of Palestine/Israel. Both its national charter and its territorial borders are laid out in the Old Testament.

Wherever they go, Jews are perpetual victims of antisemitic hostility; this is as true in the Middle East as it has been in Europe and America.

Israel is constantly threatened with annihilation at the hands of its Arab neighbors; the resurrection of European pogroms in the Middle East is a never-ending danger.

Israel must always remain on the defensive, prioritizing its perceived security needs above all else. As an exceptional nation, Israel has exceptional security demands.

Israel has always wanted to live at peace with its neighbors, but the ancient Arab hatred of Jews has made this an impossible goal.

Spreading Mythology Through Propaganda

Propaganda is a method of mass communication, or mass *persuasion*, using mass media controlled by an official elite, whether that elite consists of

17. Herzl, *Jewish State*, 56.
18. Herzl, *Jewish State*, 56.
19. Herzl, *Jewish State*, 56.
20. See the following survey of Israeli school curricula.

government officials, business executives, or a local board of education.[21] Its goal is to manufacture consent[22] throughout a population while shaping a common mindset by way of the repetitious presentation of a shared ideology. The propaganda of national mythology is accomplished most effectively through a public education system that integrates mythology into its curricula.[23] For example, Donald Yacovone's book *Teaching White Supremacy: America's Democratic Ordeal and the Forging of Our National Identity* illustrates the power and effectiveness of relaying national mythology in primary and secondary school textbooks. He carefully traces the numerous ways in which the US educational system has sustained and propagated the myth of white supremacy via its repetitious rehearsal of America's uber-myth about (white) Manifest Destiny.

Israel's first minister of education and culture (from 1951 to 1955), Ben Zion Dinur, well understood these connections between public education, propaganda, and national mythologies. As education minister, he ensured that a coherent, well-argued Zionist mythology served as the centerpiece of the entire Israeli education system.[24] Recent studies well illustrate the ongoing and willful influence of Israeli propaganda in school curricula. Nurit Peled-Elhanan's two books, *Palestine in Israeli School Books: Ideology and Propaganda in Education* and *Holocaust Education and the Semiotics of Othering in Israeli Schoolbooks*, as well as the study "'Victims of Our Own Narratives?' Portrayal of the Other in Israeli and Palestinian School Books,"[25] commissioned by the Council of Religious Institutions of the Holy Land, are good examples of recent studies describing the overt indoctrination of Zionist mythology throughout the Israeli school system. Space prohibits extensive discussion of the results of these studies. Here are a few of the salient points.

Nurit Peled-Elhanan finds Israeli school curricula suffused with mythological propaganda. Numerous examples illustrate that these materials are teaching young people to believe that:

21. See Ellul, *Propaganda*, 61, 102; Fallon, *Propaganda*, 2, 15, 23.

22. Herman and Chomsky, *Manufacturing Consent*, 1; Fallon, *Propaganda*, 32.

23. Ellul, *Propaganda*, 13; Fallon, *Propaganda*, xxiii, 65, 75.

24. For more on the important work and long-term influence of Ben Zion Dinur, see Crump, *Like Birds in a Cage*, 50–51.

25. Written by Sami Adwan, Daniel Bar-Ṭal, and Bruce E. Wexler.

Israeli Jews live under constant threat of annihilation[26] at the hands of Arabs/Palestinians who are consistently described as terrorists and troublemakers.[27] No Israeli schoolbooks contain any positive images or describe any positive aspects of Palestinian life.[28] When they are portrayed it is as agrarian wanderers accompanied by donkeys and camels.

Even more harmful prejudice is embedded in these materials, such as claims that the best solution for Israel's problems is for its Arab population to relocate and live elsewhere.[29] The goal must be to have as few Arabs as possible remaining in Israel.[30]

Appeals to the Bible are also peppered throughout the literature arguing that it proves that Jews have a right to all the land;[31] even geography textbooks emphasize the historic reality of Greater Israel.[32]

Tropes from colonial ideology are also present, such as claims that Jewish settlement in Palestine represents the arrival of Western civilization to the Middle East, whereas the Arabs represent Oriental primitivism.[33]

Whitewashing the harm done to Palestinians is regularly present, as are claims that there was no intentional "cleansing" of the Palestinian population during the war of 1947–1949;[34] the so-called Nakba was merely a spontaneous, "panicked escape" of the population from the dangers of war.[35] In fact, some schoolbooks have been discontinued because they dared to mention "ethnic cleansing."[36]

The authors of "Victims of Our Own Narratives?" present similar points of Zionist mythology in their analysis of Israeli textbooks. Describing Israel's mythology as a "collective master narrative," Jewish students are taught that:

26. Peled-Elhanan, *Palestine*, 21, 73, 92, 107.

27. Peled-Elhanan, *Palestine*, 54, 63, 73, 90, 92, 96.

28. Peled-Elhanan, *Palestine*, 49, 107.

29. Peled-Elhanan, *Palestine*, 52–53.

30. Peled-Elhanan, *Palestine*, 79.

31. Peled-Elhanan, *Palestine*, 104–7.

32. Peled-Elhanan, *Palestine*, 119. The borders of Greater Israel include parts of Egypt, Jordan, Syria, and Lebanon.

33. Peled-Elhanan, *Palestine*, 62, 98.

34. Peled-Elhanan, *Palestine*, 80, 83.

35. Peled-Elhanan, *Palestine*, 61–62, 79–80, 84, 86.

36. Peled-Elhanan, *Palestine*, 23.

The Bible teaches that Jews have "an eternal right" to all the land promised to them.[37]

Arabs are gripped by an ancient hatred of Jews.[38]

Israel is continually threatened with annihilation on all sides.[39]

Israel requires a strong posture of self-defense since it is the continual victim of Arab aggression.[40]

Israel has never wanted anything but peace with its neighbors.[41]

These studies reach identical conclusions about the role of Zionist mythology in Israel's educational system: It is uniform and all pervasive, as all good propaganda should be.[42] Particularly interesting in "Victims of Our Own Narratives?" is the attention they give to reviewing the way both Palestinian and Israeli schoolbooks treat each other's retelling of the history of Israel and Palestine. Examples are provided to illustrate the Palestinian perspectives on history that Israelis see as objectionable, even antisemitic.[43] The differences boil down to the variations in perspective that exist between the new and the old historiographies on the birth of Israel (chapters 3 and 4). In other words, what Palestinian textbooks find objectionable and Israeli textbooks find objectionable are quite the opposite of each other and map well against the older historiography and the newer understanding of Israeli origins as described by scholars known as the "new historians." These very different understandings of Israel's founding are the difference between an uncritical acceptance of historical mythology and a more mature and difficult recounting that faces those parts of the Israeli history that are unflattering, including those that burst the Zionist ideological bubble. One short, "objectionable" excerpt taken from a Palestinian history textbook will be enough to illustrate the issues at stake:

> Facilitating Jewish migration to Palestine to turn it into a Jewish state after evacuating or exterminating its people, and before this Zionist imperialist plan. . . . The struggle with the Mandate

37. Adwan et al., "Victims," 23.
38. Adwan et al., "Victims," 18.
39. Adwan et al., "Victims," 15, 18, 23, 29.
40. Adwan et al., "Victims," 14, 19, 32.
41. Adwan et al., "Victims," 14–15, 29, 39.
42. Fallon, *Propaganda*, 57.
43. Adwan et al., "Victims," 19–21, 23–25.

> government and Zionism continued until the Nakba (Catastrophe) took place in 1948. . . . Zionist gangs usurped Palestine and displaced its people from their cities, villages, land, and houses, and founded the state of Israel.[44]

The problem with citing such an example of language that Israelis find objectionable or antisemitic is that, according to an understanding of Israel's history related by the more rigorous and grounded new historians, these excerpts offer a very accurate description of the nation's founding. My eyes do not see any historical inaccuracies here. I do notice, however, that neither its perspective nor its vocabulary are in line with the ideological necessities of Zionist mythology. Therefore, Israeli censors argue that these six lines must be eliminated from the schoolbooks used to teach history to Palestinian students. In other words, from Israel's perspective there is only one way to teach the history of Palestine/Israel and that is the propagandistic way characteristic of Israeli textbooks. Any departure from the well-rehearsed contours of the Zionist, national mythology must be erased.

As striking as this example may be, it should not surprise us.

Such ideological and pedagogical rigidity is a predictable fruit of propaganda, especially when repeating the reigning national myths. Its purpose is to promote individual conformity to a society's one, true way of being. Naturally, such reigning myths can grow, displaying some measure of flexibility as new "facts" come to light, as current events raise new permutations on old questions. But this evolution in the national story must always remain coherent with the unchangeable religious value of the nation's founding myth, presenting the one, true way—the sacred way—to proceed in life.[45] After all, propaganda's objective is to manufacture consent, to "regiment the public mind,"[46] not to encourage diversity or independence. Therefore, any divergence from the traditional mythology must be criticized and eliminated wherever it is found.[47] The national myth must always remain recognizable as the nation's one and only founding myth. And loyalty to that myth is forever the desired fruit of proper education and public civility.

But, of course, Israeli schools are not the only places where Zionist mythology is cultivated. Israeli propaganda offices work overtime to sell

44. Drawn from Adwan et al., "Victims," 19,

45. Ellul, *Propaganda*, 31.

46. Fallon, *Propaganda*, 34.

47. Fallon, *Propaganda*, 28.

Zionist mythology around the world through content creation made available to every form of public and private media. Israel's National Public Diplomacy Directorate, the Israeli Government Advertising Agency, Ministry of Foreign Affairs, Ministry of Diaspora Affairs and Combatting Antisemitism are only a few of the many outlets, institutes, and training centers that not only produce propaganda material (called *hasbara* in Hebrew) but also equip young people, particularly college students, in knowing how to engage the public debate over Zionist mythology and emerge victorious.[48]

It is not hard to understand how church-going Christian Zionists become avid consumers of this Israeli propaganda, allowing themselves to be completely enfolded in the Zionist national myth, making it their own. Gary Burge has written an important article on this issue explaining the process by which Christian Zionism has absorbed, or been absorbed by, the propaganda of Israeli Zionist mythology such that Christian Zionism has become a thoroughly baptized, church-going mythology in its own right.[49] The chapters ahead will offer numerous stories illustrating just how effective Israeli propaganda has been among American evangelicals.

What Lies Ahead

The body of this book will tackle six myths playing a crucial role in filling out the evangelical Christian church's unquestioning loyalty to Israel and its Zionist mythology. In choosing which elements of this mythology to focus on, I have drilled down on those that are most important to the Zionist stories about the creation and the maintenance of the Israeli state:

Chapter One—Myth #1: Modern Israel Is the Direct Descendant of Biblical Israel

Chapter Two—Myth #2: The Bible Literally Predicts Israel's Reestablishment in the Promised Land

Chapter Three—Myth #3: The Israel–Palestine Conflict Is Rooted in Ancient Arab Antisemitism

Chapter Four—Myth #4: Israel's Victory over the Arab States in 1948 Was a Miracle

48. For an extensive discussion of the ways in which Israel infuses American civil society with Zionist propaganda, see Pappé, *Lobbying for Zionism*, 405–30.

49. Burge, "Christian Zionism as Mythology."

Introduction—Zionist Mythology, Israeli Propaganda, and Christian Zionism

Chapter Five—Myth #5: Israel's Military Is the Most Moral Army in the World

Chapter Six—Myth #6: The War Against Gaza Is a Just War of Self-Defense

The first three chapters look at matters of biblical interpretation, illustrating how different approaches to Bible reading can be used to bolster political ideology. Sometimes debates over the proper reading of Scripture are good faith discussions about the correct translation of a certain word or the significance of an unusual grammatical construction. But at other times such debates become important because of the way a certain interpretation is being milked for its political or social significance. In the case of Christian Zionism, I believe it is legitimate to talk about the weaponization of Scripture as its interpretation is harnessed to the cause of Zionist propaganda, thereby transforming Zionist myth into Christian theology.

Chapters 4, 5, and 6 look at the role of the Israeli military in establishing and defending Israel—that exceptional nation-state always in need of exceptional "security guarantees" no matter how oppressive their effects may be for others. The reader may notice a distinct change in both my argument and emphasis in this second half of the book. Christian Zionism is an eclectic movement that borrows from several different sources. The shape of the subject matter must determine the shape of the investigation. Insofar as it is "Christian," the Bible has a central role to play in informing the details of Christian Zionist belief. Chapters 1 through 3 have engaged with a few of the most important scriptural questions where the tools of biblical interpretation have a key role to play. On the other hand, insofar as this movement is "Zionist," it also adheres closely to the nationalistic, Zionist mythology disseminated through Israeli propaganda. Engaging this facet of Christian Zionism requires a look at the historical resources, comparing different schools of historical interpretation, and paying attention to the applications of Zionist myth to contemporary events. Chapters 4 through 6 will attempt to unpack three such historical questions that have become dear to the heart of American Christian Zionists.

Of course, there are various matters of Zionist mythology that could have been included here but were not. Any study like this must draw its boundaries somewhere. Also, recent developments in Gaza and the West Bank have rendered certain questions obsolete. For instance, now that Israel has obliterated the Gaza Strip and members of the Israeli Knesset are urging their government officially to annex the West Bank,[50] debates about Israel's military occupation over these territories seems a moot point. The IDF clearly possesses both regions on behalf of the state. The West Bank has already been effectively annexed as Israeli-controlled territory, filled with nearly one million Jewish settlers, containing small Palestinian "reservations" dotted throughout. The West Bank truly is best described now as looking like a piece of Swiss cheese, with Palestinians rounded up and consigned to the scattered holes.

The Myth of an Israeli Desire for Peace

There is, however, one additional myth worth touching upon before moving into the body of the book. It concerns the moribund peace process that died a silent death after the Clinton-led negotiations at Camp David in the year 2000. Subsequent attempts at negotiation between Israel and the Palestinian leadership under presidents George W. Bush and Barack Obama have gone nowhere. At least publicly, responsibility for the stalemate is never shared between the two parties but is inevitably laid solely at the feet of the Palestinians—this in itself should be sufficient evidence to make a critical thinker suspicious. In 1973, following the Geneva Peace Process, Israeli negotiator Abba Eban famously remarked that "the Arabs never miss an opportunity to miss an opportunity," relieving Israel of any responsibility for the failure of these negotiations. This refrain has been repeated many times since, shifting the responsibility from the Arabs in general to the Palestinians in particular. Now the motto focuses on them specifically—that is, the Palestinians never miss an opportunity to miss an opportunity for peace. Or alternatively the Israelis claim that "they have no partner for peace."

The Israeli–Palestinian so-called peace negotiations have offered the most public venue, and one of the most successful examples, of the persuasive power of Zionist propaganda. For whereas the repeated Israeli complaint about the absence of any Palestinian partner for peace certainly fits within the established parameters of Zionist mythology, in no way does it represent the truth of the matter. In fact, this Zionist charge turns the real history of Israeli–Palestinian peace negotiations completely upside down, standing reality on its head—a very propagandistic thing to do. The fact that so many have come to accept the Israeli narrative about repeated

50. For example, see Boxerman, "Far-Right Israeli Minister."

negotiations "failing" because the Palestinians are uninterested in peace is a testament, not to Palestinian hard-heartedness, but to the persuasive powers of Israel's well-orchestrated propaganda campaigns.

The story of Israeli foreign minister Ezer Weizman illustrates the truth being subverted in Israel's official narrative. Yet, his story is seldom, if ever, heard because his story does not fit within the framework of Zionist mythology. Weizman was Israel's chief negotiator with the Palestinians under Israeli prime minister Menachem Begin. His efforts followed on after Begin and Egypt's leader, Anwar Sadat, signed the Camp David Accords with President Jimmy Carter in 1978. Yet, Weizman's subsequent efforts to negotiate Palestinian autonomy (more on this in a moment) directly with sympathetic Palestinian representatives was consistently sabotaged by several of Begin's cabinet ministers. Publicly, Begin favored Palestinian autonomy; he proposed it; it was his idea. Privately, however, he never stopped working to stop it. Finally, in May of 1980, an exasperated Weizman had no recourse but to resign. After delivering his resignation letter to the prime minister's office, Weizman tore down a peace poster from the hallway outside and shouted at the top of his lungs, "No one here wants peace!"[51]

Ezer Weizman's story tells the truth about Israel's efforts at genuine peace negotiations with Palestinian leaders. It has always been a sham. Begin set the standards that governed Israel's peace negotiations for as long as they continued.[52] First, neither Begin nor any of his successors would ever agree to a permanent freeze on new Jewish settlements in the West Bank. Thus, the stage was set for the often heard, humorous analogy that negotiating with Israel was like negotiating over the distribution of a pizza while one side kept devouring as many slices as possible.

Begin's second principle concerned Palestinian "autonomy," not sovereignty mind you, but autonomy within the occupied territories.[53] The difference between these two is crucial. Palestinian autonomy concerns people but not land, the population but not the territory. So, the Palestinian Authority (commonly called the PA) is free to govern the Palestinian people (but not the Jewish settlers!) of the West Bank, but it has no authority over the territory. (However, even in its governance over the

51. Shlaim, *Iron Wall*, 383.

52. R. Khalidi, *Brokers*, 24.

53. Amit and Levit, *Israeli Rejectionism*, 90, 93, 95–96; Anziska, *Preventing Palestine*, 24, 12–15, 156–59, 171, 293–94; Aruri, *Dishonest Broker*, 64, 91, 115–16; R. Khalidi, *Brokers*, 1, 57, 13–15, 19–23, 51–53, 58–61, 105–6.

population—eventually granted by the Oslo Accords in 1993[54]—the Palestinian Authority remains firmly under Israel's supervision.) The land itself will always remain under Israeli control. Thus, Israel controls the borders, the natural resources, the air space and maintains the right to annex Palestinian land at will—hence, the never-ending expansion of illegal Israeli settlements throughout the West Bank. Granting Palestinian sovereignty would entail the creation of a Palestinian state; something that Menachem Begin and his successors have always said they would never allow.[55] Historian Seth Anziska concludes that Israel's unbroken commitment to Begin's rule of Palestinian autonomy "became the ground upon which the Israeli government cemented indefinite control over the occupied territories."[56] Today, Benjamin Netanyahu continues to enforce Israel's historic negotiating position in line with his Likud political party platform, which states, "The government [of Israel] will oppose the establishment of an independent Palestinian state" (article 3).[57] In other words, Palestinians will never be granted control over their own land no matter how long they negotiate.

Thus, Israel has always negotiated in such a way as to maintain its *sovereignty* over the occupied territories while publicly granting Palestinians only limited *autonomy* within the confines of Israeli control. The public remains largely unaware of this distinction, which remains a major victory for Israel's propaganda machine. For all of Israel's protestations about the many "generous offers" it has made to the Palestinians, all of which have been stubbornly refused by obdurate, unreasonable Palestinian negotiators, the truth of the matter is that *none* of these offers—not one—have included the terms that Palestinians consider most essential to their freedom: national sovereignty over their own independent state.

A sovereign Palestinian state has never been among Israel's "generous" table offerings.

A wealth of historical literature exists explaining the counter-narrative I am providing here, a counter-narrative which contests the ubiquitous Israeli propaganda about Palestinians never missing an opportunity to miss an opportunity. Despite the fact that Israel may have won the propaganda

54. R. Khalidi, *Brokers*, 59.

55. Shlaim, *Iron Wall*, 382.

56. Anziska, *Preventing Palestine*, 294.

57. Similarly, the Likud party platform of Menachem Begin's day (March 1977) declared, "Judea and Samaria will not be handed over to any foreign administration. Between the sea and the Jordan River there will be only Israeli sovereignty"; see R. Khalidi, *Brokers*, 1.

battle, the fact of the matter is that *it is the Palestinians who've never had an honest partner for peace.* Anyone wishing to contest this claim must first engage the full spectrum of historical works on the subject, including such analyses as: Salman Amit and Daphna Levit, *Israeli Rejectionism: A Hidden Agenda in the Middle East Peace Process*; Seth Anziska, *Preventing Palestine: A Political History from Camp David to Oslo*; Naseer H. Aruri, *Dishonest Broker: The U.S. Role in Israel and Palestine*; Rashid Khalidi, *Brokers of Deceit: How the US Has Undermined Peace in the Middle East*; Padraig O'Malley, *The Two-State Delusion: Israel and Palestine—A Tale of Two Narratives*; Clayton E. Swisher, *The Truth About Camp David.*

No discussion of the peace process is complete nowadays without mentioning the importance of the Palestine Papers. In January 2011 the Al Jazeera Network, together with *The Guardian* newspaper in the UK, began publishing over sixteen hundred confidential files of Palestinian negotiation documents that had come into their possession. The documents included the minutes of high-level meetings between representatives of the Palestinian Authority, Israel, and the USA stretching from 1999 to 2010.[58] The revelations were startling. Many Palestinians were shocked at the extensive concessions offered by the PA in its attempts to satisfy Israeli demands. Some concluded that the PA was nothing more than "a puppet regime for the Israeli occupation,"[59] demonstrating that Israel really *did* have a serious partner for peace if only Israel was willing to offer any concessions of its own.[60] The editor of the collection concluded that "the main story [of these papers] is of the futile and pathetic attempts by the Palestinian Authority to do almost anything to show that it is an acceptable negotiating partner."[61] Of course, Israel never failed to take advantage. For instance, Israel's refusal to place a permanent freeze on new Jewish settlement blocks in the West Bank is a recurring theme of discussion. At one point, the Israeli negotiator, Tzipi Livni, even admitted that the "Israeli policy is to take more and more land day after day, and that at the end of the day we'll say that it is impossible, we already have the land, and we cannot create the [Palestinian] state."[62]

58. These files are now available in the book *The Palestine Papers* by Swisher.

59. Swisher, *Palestine Papers*, 18.

60. Swisher, *Palestine Papers*, 20.

61. Swisher, *Palestine Papers*, 23.

62. Swisher, *Palestine Papers*, 15, 34; it is unclear whether Livni intended merely to parrot Palestinian complaints. In any case, she neither rejects nor condemns the claim

In other words, the so-called peace negotiations were always a colossal PR exercise intended to undergird Zionist mythology. The public goal was to whitewash Israel's reputation as the one continually seeking peace with its recalcitrant Arab neighbors while simultaneously black-balling Palestinians as the perennial foot-draggers determined to avoid peace at all costs. Privately, as the Palestine Papers demonstrate, Israel's ultimate goal was to forestall any developments that might even hint at the remote possibility of a future, sovereign Palestinian state.

Propaganda, Peace, and Pacification

The long history of failed peace negotiations is just one more plotline in the complex web of intersecting narratives that make up the national story of Zionist mythology. Another confusion that this plotline helps to uncover is the divergent perspectives on "peace" separating Israeli from Palestinian negotiators. Unfortunately, a common vocabulary does not guarantee common goals or shared understandings. In fact, it may provide another wedge issue for propagandists to exploit.

At the heart of this problem lay two different understandings of peace. Israel's definition of peace has always meant *domination without dissent*. As long as Israel remained the dominant occupier and Palestinians continued to acquiesce in their role as the subdued subordinates, then the Israelis believed they would have "peace." Theirs is a thoroughly colonial understanding of peace as pacification, peace for the colonizers if not for the colonized. Thus, an effective peace plan will ensure that the natives never become restless no matter the injustices done to them.

The Palestinians, on the other hand, understand that true peace is always the fruit of justice. As long as the colonial roles of occupied and occupier continue to exist in Israel–Palestine, there can be no such thing as authentic peace between Israelis and Palestinians. For there is no justice in a place where one group dominates another in their own land, where a system of structural violence defines some as occupiers and others as occupied. There can be no genuine peace as long as a Jewish supremacist ethnostate consigns native Palestinians to second-class status, forever denying them the rights of self-determination that Israel clings to so vociferously for itself.

---

being made.

Justice is a prerequisite to real peace. All talk about peace without justice is a mockery of the concept. Israel must come to understand this lesson for any future peace negotiations finally to become successful in the long term. Many who call themselves peacemakers apparently fail to grasp this issue. Thus, their ostensible efforts at peacemaking offer little more than sandcastles built in an Israeli sandbox. Until Israel chooses to renounce the racist ideology of political Zionism, to deconstruct its apartheid, ethnocratic state, and to grant all Palestinians equal rights in a liberal democracy that extends equal opportunity to all its citizens, there can be no genuine, lasting peace in Israel–Palestine.

Though Israel has mastered the art of stage-managing public perceptions of reality through massive propaganda campaigns, the realities of injustice can never be expunged. Even if the anti-propaganda demands—represented by this book, for example—for true justice in Palestine ultimately fail to prevail, continuing to call for Palestinian freedom may help to open more eyes to the realities of life in Israel–Palestine. Perhaps one day enough people, Americans in particular, will see through the propaganda and begin to testify to the unvarnished truth, insisting that Israel be treated as the pariah state that it truly is.

MYTH #1

Modern Israel Is the Direct Descendent of Biblical Israel

My wife and I never imagined that we'd be assaulted for being peace activists. But it happened during our last visit to Washington, DC. After driving to Detroit from Grand Rapids, Michigan, we rode a bus to our nation's capital with other pro-Palestinian peace activists in order to march through the Washington Mall with the organization End the Occupation. We were demanding that the US government rescind its support for Israel's illegal military occupation of the West Bank and the Gaza Strip. We have friends living in a Palestinian refugee camp near Bethlehem, only a few miles from Jerusalem. We had witnessed for ourselves the daily humiliations that they endured under the oppressive regimen imposed by the Israeli soldiers who walked daily through their streets.

We marched from the Washington Monument to the Lincoln Memorial chanting and carrying our banners demanding Palestinian liberation. When the march had ended my wife and I took a break and rested on a nearby patch of grass to eat our sack lunches. Our upright sign, Free Palestine, was stuck in the dirt next to us as we ate. Occasionally a passerby would stop to talk, asking us what we were doing. One especially grumpy-looking old man didn't stop to ask questions but swung his cane (near my wife's head) to hit our sign as he passed by. Raising his voice he declared, "America would be nothing without Israel!" Continuing to walk on, he didn't stop to explain how this opinion related to the question of Palestinian freedom. But I could guess.

Though I seriously doubt that he had the Bible in mind as he swung his cane through the air, my elderly attacker had expressed a Jewish Zionist version of a Christian Zionist belief based on the biblical book of Genesis. Rooting their logic in Genesis chapter 12 verse 3, Christian Zionists commonly insist that "God blesses those who bless Israel and curses those who curse Israel." Apparently, every nation's destiny depends on its foreign policy toward the modern Israeli nation-state. Recording the Lord's announcement to the patriarch Abraham, the biblical text says,

> I will bless those who bless you,
> and whoever curses you I will curse;
> and all the peoples on earth will be blessed through you.

The seventh Earl of Shaftesbury, Lord Ashley (1801–1885), a prominent leader among nineteenth-century British evangelicals, was "the first politician of stature" to work toward a Jewish return to the land of Palestine.[1] Believing that the Jewish people were "the apple of God's eye," Lord Shaftesbury was also among the first to develop an overview of European history that placed the fate of the Jews center-stage. God treated the nations of the world as they treated Israel. On his view, for example, the Spanish empire had fallen, i.e., was cursed by God, because Spain evicted its Jewish population in 1492, banishing them from the country. On the other hand, English economic fortunes began to rise, i.e., were blessed by God, as soon as that nation opened its doors to welcome stateless Jewish immigrants.[2]

The 1917 edition of the Scofield Reference Bible,[3] complete with footnotes providing theological (and dispensationalist) commentary, is one of the founding documents of American Christian Zionism. Concerning Gen 12:3, Scofield wrote that God's warning about blessing and cursing is "wonderfully fulfilled in the history of the dispersion. It has invariably fared ill with the people who have persecuted the Jew—well with those who have protected him."[4] The post-Holocaust 1967 Scofield edition adds the warning, "For a nation to commit the sin of anti-Semitism brings inevitable

1. D. Lewis, *Origins*, 107.

2. D. Lewis, *Origins*, 169.

3. The Scofield Bible became a key reference point for both American dispensationalists and Christian Zionists. C. I. Scofield wrote a lengthy series of footnotes and theological explanations appended to the King James Version of the biblical text. Reading Scripture through the lens of dispensational theology, Scofield highlighted the connection between Israel's literal return to their ancient "homeland" and the second coming of Christ.

4. Scofield, *Scofield Reference Bible*, 25.

judgment."[5] Illustrating the apparent veracity of this biblical guarantee—and the way in which it serves as empirical evidence for both God's existence as well as his sovereignty over world history—has become a standard feature of Christian Zionist apologetics. Zionist preachers continue to shape their own idiosyncratic surveys of world history by explaining how nations and empires either prosper or decline depending on their treatment of the Jews.[6]

Of course, using Gen 12:3 in this way involves a number of debatable assumptions, the most fundamental being whether or not God's promise to the man Abraham automatically translates into an open-ended pledge that carries on to the modern nation-state. The promise of blessings and curses, including the promise of a new land to occupy, is handed on to Abraham's descendants, first to Isaac and Jacob (Gen 12:1–7; 27:26–29; 28:3–4) and eventually to the entire people of Israel (Num 24:8–10).[7] But the questions remain: Does modern Israel stand in line to inherit the promises made to Old Testament Israel? Is the modern Jewish state composed of the descendants of Abraham?[8] Furthermore, how does the New Testament evidence fit into answering these questions about Israel's status today?

The Apostle Paul's Answer to the Question of Identity

For the sake of space, I will limit my discussion to the apostle Paul's perspective on the seed of Abraham as it is laid out in the New Testament books of Galatians and Romans. For a fuller discussion of the biblical evidence, I suggest reading Gary Burge's excellent book *Jesus and the Land: The New Testament Challenge to "Holy Land" Theology*.[9] In this chapter and the next we will discover that *the New Testament engages in a major*

5. Scofield, *New Scofield Reference Bible*, 19.

6. For numerous examples, see Spector, *Evangelicals and Israel*, 23–35.

7. For a good analysis of the trajectory of these promises throughout Scripture, see Fisk, "Genesis 12:3," 144–63.

8. How best to determine individual Jewish identity for inclusion in the Jewish state has been a long-term debate in Israeli society; see Orr, *unJewish State*. Controversy focuses on whether religion or ethnicity forms the basis of Jewish identity. For those who insist on a religious basis of identity, "the Zionist vision of a new Jewish identity [in Israel] produced Hebrew-speaking Gentiles who have little in common with traditional Judaism" (218). For these people, the so-called "Jewish state" is *not*, by and large, composed of Jews.

9. Also see Dalrymple, *These Brothers of Mine*.

project of redefinition. By reading the Old Testament backward through the lens of faith in Jesus and his ministry, the apostles redefine what it means to be a descendant of Abraham and a member of God's covenant community. This happens not because the New Testament is somehow prioritized over the Old Testament. Rather, it is a result of reading all the Bible holistically, paying attention to how the Old and New Testaments interact. We must learn to read the Bible twice, first from front to back and then from back to front. On a first reading, we learn about God's dealings with the people of Israel, the arrival of Israel's messiah, and the life of the community Jesus leaves behind after his ascension. On the second reading, we learn about the apostles' *rereading* of that Old Testament story in the light of Christ's life, death, resurrection, and ascension. A failure to take that second, crucial rereading of the Old Testament in light of Christ's earthly ministry with sufficient seriousness is the fatal flaw in Christian Zionist Bible reading. It is one of the principal reasons why they misunderstand the relevance or irrelevance of Gen 12:3 to modern Israel. We will discuss these interpretive issues more fully in chapter 2.

The Descendants of Abraham According to Galatians

Paul's Letter to the Galatians was prompted by a controversy stirred up within the local church by a group he refers to as "the circumcision party," sometimes called the Judaizers (Gal 2:12). The evidence indicates that this Judaizing group insisted that gentile converts to the Christian faith could only be considered genuine believers if they also took on the signs of Jewish religion. In their view, just as the messiah was Jewish, and just as the earliest members of the Christ-community were Jewish, so gentile believers in the messiah must also become Jewish by observing Torah and submitting to circumcision.

Paul, however, wanted nothing to do with this blend of Christian faith mixed with a necessary adherence to Jewish traditions and Old Testament law. In fact, Paul is flabbergasted that the Galatians are considering such things:[10]

> I am astonished that you are so quickly deserting the one who called you by the grace of Christ and are turning to a different gospel—which is really no gospel at all. . . . If anyone is preaching

10. For similar warnings and corrections, see Gal 5:2, 7–12; 6:12–15.

> to you a gospel other than what you accepted, let him be eternally condemned! (Gal 1:6–9)

Paul begins his corrective argument by explaining how God made Abraham the model of faith in Christ without any commitment to Jewish practices (Gal 3:6–19).[11] Abraham was, in fact, the original gentile believer in the gospel. Beginning from Gen 15:6, cited in Gal 3:6, Paul reminded his readers that Abraham was considered "righteous" by faith alone before he was circumcised, an event that occurred in Gen 17. *Thus, Abraham became the prototypical, uncircumcised gentile believer!* In fact, God's words to Abraham in Gen 12:3—"All nations will be blessed through you"—were the original announcement of the New Testament gospel to the world (Gal 3:8). Here was the first formulation of the good news promising justification (that is, divine "blessing") by faith alone apart from works of the law. In a few brief sentences, the apostle has redefined what it means to be a descendant of Abraham, the lynchpin of Jewish identity. Since the advent of Jesus Christ, that lineage is traced by way of trust in and adherence to Jesus as Lord and Savior—something that is equally true for Jews and non-Jews alike. Even the physical descendants of Abraham are truly made Abraham's spiritual descendants by faith. Neither adherence to Torah, circumcision, nor citizenship in a territorial nation-state have anything to do with Paul's new formulation of personal identity.

The next section of Gal 3 continues this crucial theme. Paul initiates his argument by beginning at the end: Everyone who trusts in Christ is Abraham's descendant. Having started at the conclusion, he then takes a step back and clarifies an essential, prior step in his logic. Verse 16 lays out this preceding step: "The promises were spoken to Abraham and his seed. Scripture does not say 'and to seeds,' meaning many people, but 'and to your seed,' meaning one person, who is Christ." In other words, the true heir of God's promises to Abraham was not Isaac, Jacob, the nation of Israel, or even the collection of individual Christians; the real heir is Christ alone. He is the singular seed. Believers in the resurrected Jesus become joint-heirs of God's promise by their incorporation into Christ. By faith we participate in Jesus' "seed-hood," if you will. Paul underscores the full measure of his logic in verse 29—"*If* you belong to Christ, *then* you are Abraham's seed, and heirs according to the promise" (emphasis added). In this regard, all are alike. There is "neither Jew nor Gentile" (v. 28). Only faith-based grafting

11. For a more extensive discussion of Gal 3:6–9 and its role in Christian Zionist apologetics, see Crump, *Like Birds in a Cage*, 177–86.

into Christ, that is "union with Christ," establishes any meaningful descent from Abraham. Theirs alone are the promises.

In contrast to Paul's argument in Gal 3, Christian Zionists insist that the Old Testament must only be interpreted and applied after a superficial reading of the text, which ignores how the New Testament writer is using the passage for his own purposes.[12] By this way of thinking, whatever Gen 12:3 and its numerous iterations meant literally in its original Old Testament context yields the complete understanding of what the text may refer to today. Genesis 12 must denote only physical descendants living in a physical piece of real estate. Furthermore, this adherence to literalistic interpretation is essential to Christian Zionist thinking as it safeguards God's faithfulness to his promises. In other words, if God promises to give people X, then a faithful, promise-keeping God must literally give people X. If God does otherwise, why should anyone believe any of God's promises?

Galatians 3, however, makes it painfully obvious that Paul did not abide by our modern rules of Bible reading. Paul was interested in doing something very different with Gen 12. He interpreted the Old Testament through Christ—and this is what we see the New Testament doing again and again. Neither are God's actions limited to the paths we imagine are logically necessary to protect divine faithfulness. Both constraints are appealed to by Christian Zionists, but these impositions muzzle Paul's Spirit-inspired exposition. Paul comes to understand Gen 12:3 in a manner we'd least expect. Under the inspiration of the Holy Spirit, Paul discovers that the deepest meaning of Gen 12:3 lies elsewhere. And he shows no signs of worry that his reinterpretation of Gen 12:3 will threaten belief in divine faithfulness. God's faithfulness is now revealed in Jesus of Nazareth—not Isaac or Jacob or national Israel—sent to be Abraham's solitary seed. New covenant believers of all stripes are now counted as Abraham's descendants through the single seed that is Christ alone. I cannot imagine a more surprising way to interpret Gen 12. Paul is clearly rereading, reinterpreting, reframing, the Old Testament story via the inspiration of the Spirit of prophecy, viewing it afresh through the lens of Jesus' life and ministry. The way of the gospel becomes the unanticipated avenue for God to demonstrate faithfulness to father Abraham.

12. See the discussion of Christian Zionism's literalistic readings of the New Testament in Crump, *Like Birds in a Cage*, 16–17, 94–97, 105.

The Descendants of Abraham According to Romans

The book of Romans returns to Paul's argument in Gal 3 about Abraham and his descendants. In sending this letter to the capital city of Rome, Paul is testing the waters for his relocation to the center of the empire. Paul is thinking about making Rome his home base in the next phase of his missionary enterprise as he hopes to move westward into Europe. But will the Christian community in Rome support his continued outreach as apostle to the gentiles? Or is there a sizable enough contingent of the Judaizing party in the Roman church to make the capital city an inhospitable place to base his operations? Paul hopes to clear the way for a friendly welcome by explaining his theology of gentile inclusion among the descendants of Abraham.

Omitting any reference to Gen 12, Paul promotes Gen 15:6 as the premier text rooting his argument in Old Testament precedent. Paul either quotes or refers to this text eight times throughout Rom 4 (vv. 3, 5, 9, 11, 13, 22, 23, 24). Two of these references form an "inclusio" framing Paul's argument. An inclusio serves as thematic bookends marking the opening (v. 3) and the closing (vv. 22–24) of a discussion, underlining its central concern. Verse 3 introduces the pivotal issue, "What does scripture say? 'Abraham believed God, and it was credited to him as righteousness.'" Verses 22–24 draw Paul's argument to a close by summarizing the relevance of Gen 15:6 for all who believe:

> This is why "it was credited to him as righteousness." The words "it was credited to him" were written not for him alone, but also for us to whom God will "credit righteousness"—for us who believe in him who raised Jesus our Lord from the dead.

The final line punctuates the content of the faith Paul has been referring to throughout the preceding verses; it is specifically faith in Jesus of Nazareth, the crucified, resurrected Lord.

The body of Paul's argument expands upon the theme of faith apart from works of the law introduced in Gal 3. Abraham's fatherhood is mentioned seven times (vv. 1, 11, 12, 16, 17 [twice], 18). Once again, his offspring are Jews and gentiles distinguished by their faith in Jesus. Romans 4:9a introduces the pivotal question of who will have their faith credited to them as righteousness (vv. 4–8): "Is this blessedness only for the circumcised, or also for the uncircumcised?" (v. 9b). Paul highlights Abraham's fatherhood first for uncircumcised gentiles, since "Abraham's faith was credited to him as righteousness" before he was circumcised in Gen 17 (vv. 9b–11). But Abraham is also the father of *believing* Jews, "the circumcised who not only are circumcised but who also follow in the footsteps of the faith that our father Abraham had before he was circumcised" (v. 12). The key for both parties is faith not physical descent. In this way, Abraham is "made the father of many nations" (v. 17).

But not only has Abraham's faith, replicated among the gentiles, come to include many peoples from around the world; so also has it embraced the lands and territories those gentiles inhabit. By faith "Abraham and his offspring received the promise that he would be *heir of the world*" (v. 13)—not Judea, Samaria, the land of Canaan, or Israel, but the entire earth. Just as Paul in Galatians restricted the reference of Abraham's "seed" to Jesus alone, so now in Romans he enlarges the reference to promised real estate to include all the world. Paul's Spirit-inspired vision now encompasses the globe as the promised inheritance for all those, Jew and gentile alike, who believe in Jesus.

Following Paul's argument is not a matter of "spiritualizing" the text. Nor is it an exercise in allegorizing or diminishing the value of the Old Testament with respect to the New. It does not arise from a philosophical preference for universalism over historical particularity. Rather, Paul once again is rereading the story of Abraham from back to front by looking through the lens of Jesus' life and work. This new lens includes Jesus' continuing work through the Spirit within his new covenant community—something Paul witnessed firsthand day in and day out. As a result, Paul shows no interest in anything like contemporary "holy land theology." He offers no encouragement for regathering the Jews into a reconquered territory between the Mediterranean Sea and the Jordan River. Israel's war of conquest in 1948 was just another bloody conflict in the long line of human tragedies spawned by ethnic nationalism and humanity's penchant for territorial conquest.

Blessings and Curses in the New Testament

We have seen that, according to the books of Galatians and Romans, God's promises to Abraham are inherited by all those, Jews and gentiles, who trust in the resurrected Jesus Christ.[13] Physical descent does not factor into this

13. I am convinced that the remainder of the New Testament evidence agrees with Paul's conclusions in Galatians and Romans; see Burge, *Jesus and the Land*; Crump, *Like*

equation. Thus, the promise of land is reinterpreted in the same way. God now promises the entire world as an inheritance to all those who believe in Jesus. Therefore, God's promise of land does not carry over to the modern nation-state of Israel, for there is no line of (spiritual) continuity between ancient and modern Israel. That prior line of connection was reconfigured by Jesus, and according to Paul, the spiritual connection forged by faith is what matters most.

So, what about the promises of blessings and curses in Gen 12:3? If they do not pertain to modern Israel, as Christian Zionists insist, then to whom do they refer? According to the logic of Paul's argument, the promise of blessings and curses can only refer to: (a) Christ himself, the "seed" of Abraham, as well as (b) Abraham's spiritual descendants, the multiethnic church, the body of Christ. The New Testament applies this understanding of blessings and curses from Gen 12:3 in its teaching about the final judgment. Just as God's promise of protection applied to Abraham and his Old Testament descendants, so too the promise of "blessing those who bless you and cursing those who curse you" now applies to God's global family incorporated into Christ by faith. The Father pays attention to the way the world treats his children.

Paul addresses this spiritual dynamic for the first time in 1 Thess 2:14b–16:

> For you, brothers and sisters, became imitators of God's churches in Judea, which are in Christ Jesus: You suffered from your own people the same things those churches suffered from the Jews who killed the Lord Jesus and the prophets and also drove us out. They displease God and are hostile to everyone in their effort to keep us from speaking to the Gentiles so that they may be saved. In this way they always heap up their sins to the limit. The wrath of God has come upon them at last.

At different times and places both believing Jews and gentiles have suffered persecution from their compatriots who vehemently opposed the spread of the good news of Christ in their communities. They opposed the Lord directly by attempting to hinder the spread of his gospel; and they opposed Christ's church by working to stop others from joining the new community. Thus, by working "to curse" God's people, they have brought God's curse of judgment upon themselves. Accordingly, Paul warns, "The wrath of God

Birds in a Cage; Dalrymple, *Land of Contention*, 36–54.

has come upon them at last."[14] Paul does not elaborate on the details of God's judgment here and now, but the unfolding of the divine curse both temporally and eternally is inevitable.

Second Thessalonians 1:4–8 elaborates the same point:

> Therefore, among God's churches we boast about your perseverance and faith in all the persecutions and trials you are enduring. All this is evidence that God's judgment is right, and as a result you will be counted worthy of the kingdom of God, for which you are suffering. God is just: He will pay back trouble to those who trouble you and give relief to you who are troubled, and to us as well. This will happen when the Lord Jesus is revealed from heaven in blazing fire with his powerful angels. He will punish those who do not know God and do not obey the gospel of our Lord Jesus.

Again, the Father's distributive justice is revealed in the way he blesses his obedient children and pays back trouble to those who trouble faithful believers in Christ. Eternal punishment will fall upon all those who dare to curse Abraham's spiritual seed.

The book of Revelation provides the ultimate depiction of how God applies the promise of blessing to those who bless Abraham's seed and cursing against those who curse that seed. In Rev 6:9–11 all those who have been martyred "for the word of God and the testimony they had maintained" are crying out from beneath heaven's altar, asking Christ how much longer they must wait until he will "judge the inhabitants of the earth and avenge our blood?" Jesus tells them to be patient; they must wait for "the number of their fellow servants and brothers who were to be killed as they had been was completed." When the full number of Christian martyrs is complete, then the Lord will condemn all those who condemned his people, cursing those who cursed his seed.

The fullest account of this principle of judgment is found in what is perhaps the most misunderstood of Jesus' parables—the parable of the sheep and the goats (Matt 25:31–46). The meaning of this story hinges on how we understand Jesus' reference to "the least of these brothers of mine." There is a long Christian tradition of applying this description to the most oppressed and disenfranchised members of society. Jesus identifies with the world's poor, we are told. So, anyone who has helped the oppressed has also helped Jesus.

14. The words "at last" may also be translated as "fully."

The problem with this perspective, however, is that it does not interpret the phrase "the least of these my brothers" within the context of Matthew's Gospel.[15] Instead, it imposes a generalized humanitarian concern that does not arise from within the immediate context. There are many other passages where a broad-based humanitarianism is emphasized in Scripture, but Matt 25 is not one of them. Matthew's Gospel, like every Gospel, has its own narrative continuity and thematic development. Matthew must be read holistically, paying attention to how the plot unfolds from beginning to end. Jesus' claim that "when you have done it to the least of these my brothers, you have done it to me" has several components that have all previously been defined in Matthew's Gospel. We can break this phrase down into three parts: (a) when you have done it to them, you have done it to me (see Matt 10:40; 18:2–6); (b) the least of these or these little ones (see Matt 10:42; 18:2–6); (c) my brothers (see Matt 12:46–50). All three phrases point us, not to the poor or oppressed in general, but to Jesus' faithful disciples (i.e., the universal church) in particular.

Jesus makes it clear that he is talking about things that will happen at the last judgment when he returns to earth in glory—sometimes referred to as the parousia (vv. 31, 46). Humanity will be separated into two groups: the sheep and the goats. The sheep will be "blessed" (v. 34). They will inherit the eternal kingdom because they cared for the Father's children, Abraham's descendants, in their time of need joining them as brothers and sisters. The goats, on the other hand, will be "cursed," thrown into "the eternal fire prepared for the devil and his angels" (v. 41) because they did not care for God's people but made their lives more difficult by neglect. We see that God's promises about divine blessings and curses haunt human history from Abraham until its conclusion. The Lord told Abraham, "I will bless those who bless you (and your seed) and curse those who curse you (and your seed)." We now understand that the final realization of that promise is described by Jesus as occurring at the final judgment when the universal church is vindicated and introduced into God's eternal kingdom.

Conclusion

We began this chapter by asking several questions: Does modern Israel stand in line to inherit the promises made to Old Testament Israel? Is the

15. For another good analysis of this parable and its proper, contextual interpretation, see Dalrymple, *These Brothers of Mine*, 146–50.

modern Jewish state composed of the descendants of Abraham? How does the New Testament evidence fit into answering these questions about Israel's status today?

Paul's letters to Galatia and to Rome provide clear answers to these questions. First, modern Israel does not stand in line to inherit the Old Testament promises. The modern Jewish state may be partially composed of Abraham's physical descendants, but the promises God made to Abraham are now passed on to the spiritual descendants who trace their lineage through faith in Jesus Christ. Believers in Jesus now exercise the faith of Abraham, responding to the gospel message announced to Abraham long ago.

We also discover that the New Testament writers (Paul is typical in this respect) don't abide by the Christian Zionist rules of interpretation. Quite the contrary. Paul is surprisingly creative as he reinterprets the story of Abraham through the New Testament lens of Jesus' accomplishments. Abraham's seed is Christ. Abraham's descendants are all those who believe in Christ. Abraham's promised land is the entire world. The protection promised to Abraham's seed in Gen 12:3 is ultimately realized in the church on Judgment Day. All those who made life difficult for God's children will be cursed with eternal punishment; while all those who joined the church and cared for its members, especially when they suffered, will be blessed with eternal life.

An unavoidable conclusion arising from this study of the New Testament material is that the common discussion about the legitimacy of connecting the modern Israeli nation-state to ancient, biblical Israel/Judea/Samaria raises a moot point. Even if it were possible to construct a direct line of unbroken continuity from the ancient descendants of Abraham, Isaac, and Jacob to the modern Jewish community gathered in the Israeli nation-state—something I believe it is impossible to do—it would have no practical or theological significance for a Christian's evaluation of the Israeli–Palestinian conflict. Insofar as I am addressing the problems raised by *Christian* Zionism, the apostle Paul's redefinition of Abraham's descendants as "all those who believe" decidedly trumps anyone's hypothetical, historical, or sociological reconstruction of ancient Jewish patrimony in the land of Israel–Palestine.

MYTH #2

The Bible Literally Predicts Israel's Reestablishment in the Promised Land

MANY CHRISTIAN ZIONISTS APPEAR to view the Palestinian people as an unruly impediment to the fulfillment of God's promises to Abraham, an impediment that can blithely be swept aside since nothing can stand in the way of Old Testament prophetic fulfillment. In a 2005 speech, John Hagee of San Antonio, Texas, the dean of American Christian Zionism, announced that "the Palestinians have never owned the land. . . . The land of Israel was given to Abraham, Isaac and Jacob. . . . [It] belongs to the Jewish people today, tomorrow and forever."[1] Similarly, Robert Benne, emeritus professor at Roanoke College, openly advises the mass displacement of Palestinians, since "God has a continuing covenant with Israel that includes land and the promise of return. These combined special claims override even the 'natural rights' of the Palestinians to their land."[2]

Really?

Here we encounter the second myth about Israel which is closely related to the first. The majority of Christian Zionists, and a good number of Jewish Zionists, believe that the modern nation-state of Israel was established in 1948 as the fulfillment of divine promises made to the Jewish people in the Hebrew Scriptures, what Christians call the Old Testament. Such Zionists argue that just as there is a direct line of continuity from ancient, Old Testament Israel to the modern nation-state (chapter 1), so the Old Testament—when read correctly and taken literally—remains the written charter justifying Israel's existence in the Middle East today. The fact

1. Quoted in Nowlin, "Apocalypse Now," para. 65.
2. Benne, "Theology and Politics," 245–46.

that 750,000 Palestinians were brutally displaced from their homes during that war is almost inconsequential to Zionist thinking. Fulfilling God's plan is paramount.

Non-Zionist Christians, such as myself, do not share this position. I also take the Bible seriously as the word of God, but I do not find a charter for the modern Israeli nation-state in its pages. I also cannot ignore Palestinian suffering. Obviously, these two groups, Zionist and non-Zionist, are reading the Bible very differently. They also have two different understandings of biblical authority. Explaining these differences is the goal of this chapter.[3] Along the way we will discover exactly why this second myth about modern Israel is untrue.

Christian Zionist Interpretation

Literal interpretation is the crucial first ingredient in the Zionist recipe for how to read the Bible. Scripture must be taken at face value, meaning that the reader seeks to grasp the "common sense understanding" of the words on the page. This is not done naively. Proper interpretation requires knowledge of the original languages together with a grasp of the literature's historical context, cultural setting, literary genre, and structure. Scholars describe this way of reading Scripture as the grammatical-historical method. By learning the answers to these various questions about the historical and literary nature of the biblical text, the reader/interpreter seeks to allow the words of the Bible "to stand according to their plain and obvious sense."[4] The operative question is, What would this plain and obvious sense have meant to the original audience?

When addressing the New Testament fulfillment of Old Testament prophecies, literal interpretation requires a one-to-one, plain sense correspondence between prophetic details and the manner of their futuristic fulfillment. For instance, if the Old Testament says that the scattered people of Israel must return to their homeland and rebuild the temple, then these things must occur literally in our modern world. The possibility that such prophecies may have been fulfilled literally when the people of Judah returned from their Babylonian exile in 538 BC is not considered the final fulfillment that the prophets were anticipating.

3. For a fuller discussion of these issues accompanied by detailed biblical examples, see my book *Like Birds in a Cage*, 86–135, 212–19.

4. Horner, *Future Israel*, 187.

Most non-Zionists like myself also value this plain sense way of Bible reading even though we disagree about its literal application to prophetic fulfillment. Understanding the Old Testament's original plain sense meaning and significance is crucial to an accurate understanding of Scripture. The difference appears in how the method is applied to the New Testament when the apostolic writers are interpreting prophecy. Christian Zionists emphasize the importance of literalism primarily *for the Old Testament.* Rarely is a literal reading of the New Testament emphasized with the same degree of urgency, especially when the New Testament is interpreting Old Testament prophecy. For instance, Michael Vlach, professor at Master's Seminary, insists that "Old Testament texts, as understood within their historical-grammatical contexts, must be the starting point for understanding God's plans for national Israel."[5] All proper understanding begins with and never deviates from a literalistic understanding of the Old Testament.

Literal interpretation leads to the second Christian Zionist assumption, something called *antecedent theology*. The rule of antecedent theology insists that what was written first must always control or take precedence over later statements on a subject. The earliest teaching will always take priority over later teaching on the same topic. With respect to Bible reading, this means that the Old Testament always has priority over the New Testament. The New Testament can never change or amend the literal meaning of the Old Testament. The Old Testament rules the roost. For example, Michael Rydelnik, professor at Moody Bible Institute, says that "the Old Testament needs to guide the understanding of the New Testament, and not vice versa."[6] Vlach concurs, writing that "the New Testament never reinterprets or changes the original meaning of Old Testament texts, especially those that address eschatological issues regarding Israel."[7] Paul Feinberg, former professor at Trinity Evangelical Divinity School, argues that "the sense of the OT text must be determined within its historical and cultural setting, and that sense is determinative for the NT fulfilment."[8] Charles Ryrie of Dallas Theological Seminary insists that "new revelation cannot mean contradictory revelation. Later revelation on a subject does not make the earlier revelation mean something different."[9]

5. Vlach, *Church*, 124.

6. Rydelnik, "Hermeneutics of the Conflict," 71.

7. Vlach, *Church*, 123; also see 185–87.

8. P. Feinberg, "Hermeneutics of Discontinuity," 127.

9. Ryrie, *Dispensationalism*, 84, cited in Vlach, *Church*, 127.

It becomes evident that the Christian Zionist principle of antecedent theology is an effort to establish the Old Testament's theological priority.[10] A literal understanding of the Old Testament prophecies about Israel must be allowed to stand as they are *regardless of anything the New Testament authors may have to say about them.* On the rare occasion when a Christian Zionist may acknowledge that a New Testament writer does reinterpret an Old Testament passage, Old Testament priority is maintained by way of a third assumption called *the rule of double fulfillment.*[11] Since many Christian Zionists believe that Israel and the Christian church must remain separate and distinct entities as two different peoples of God,[12] it is an easy move to allow that a New Testament reinterpretation of the Old (chapter 1) may be fulfilled in the Christian church while the literal meaning of the Old Testament text waits for a future fulfillment in physical Israel. As John Feinberg, professor at Trinity Evangelical Divinity School, surmised, why shouldn't Old Testament prophecy "have one application to the church now plus a further application to national Israel in the future?"[13]

The problem with these Zionist rules of interpretation is that they are arbitrarily imposed by an authority other than the Bible. None of them are self-evident conclusions drawn from the text of Scripture. They are simply declared to be so by academic authority figures who happen to have a particular theological approach to reading Scripture. Indeed, all readers do this, but the risk appears in presenting their approach as somehow inherent within the biblical text itself without ample demonstration. Christian Zionist readers' inherent concern is to safeguard the Zionist belief in national Israel's role as the lynchpin of God's prophetic plan for the future of the world. For Christian Zionism, this geopolitical and theological vision becomes the fundamental, controlling methodology that seems to blind them to other readings encouraged by the biblical texts themselves. Thus, rather than allowing Scripture to speak for itself, the voice of the New Testament is muzzled whenever it appears to shirk the constraints of Old Testament literalism, which it often does (see below).

10. This methodology may also be motivated, in part, by a suspicion of the historical critical method and an allergic response to allegorical readings of the Old Testament.

11. J. Feinberg, "Systems of Discontinuity," 77, 81; Larsen, *Jews, Gentiles*, 51.

12. For a discussion with examples of this Zionist commitment to keep the church and Israel separate and distinct from one another, see Crump, *Like Birds in a Cage*, 178.

13. J. Feinberg, "Systems of Discontinuity," 68.

But there is a second problem created by Christian Zionism's emphasis on the priority of Old Testament teaching. This is the tension created by an unresolved disparity between Old Testament prophecies about Israel and the complete absence of any New Testament endorsement of that literalistic vision. In a rare moment of candor, Michael Vlach acknowledges this fact when he confesses that "there is no undisputed New Testament verse that explicitly states 'Israel will be restored to its land and have a special service to the nations.'"[14] Vlach has made a crucial observation. Applying the same literal, commonsense method of interpretation to the New Testament as is applied to the Old Testament yields results that diverge significantly from the one-to-one correspondence demanded by Zionist presuppositions. The Old Testament picture of literal Israel resettling its promised land, rebuilding the temple, and drawing all nations to itself is never clearly reproduced anywhere in the New Testament. This is the oddity produced by insisting on biblical, prophetic literalism: *New Testament literalism does not affirm Old Testament literalism*. Quite the opposite. This fact is the rarely acknowledged elephant in the room that Christian Zionists try to disguise with their arbitrary, illogical rules of antecedent theology and double fulfillment.[15]

Some will claim that God never needs to repeat himself; having stated something once in the Old Testament means there is no reason for God to repeat that claim in the New. Others will say that since Israel occupied the land of Judah and Herod's temple was still standing in the time of Jesus, there was no need to repeat such national prophecies. Yet, these assertions smack of special pleading. They can only prove satisfying to those who ignore the abundant evidence of New Testament *re*-interpretation presented in this and the previous chapter. Again, if the New Testament writers believed in the literal fulfillment of the Old Testament prophecies about Israel in association with the coming of Jesus, then why were they "so consistently incapable of clearly expressing what they actually meant?"[16]

14. Vlach, *Church*, 203.

15. I say these rules are illogical because they are clear examples of the logical fallacy known as *ipse dixit*; that is, they are examples of authoritative statements made with no attempt at exegetical justification.

16. Crump, *Like Birds in a Cage*, 111.

Another Way to Read Scripture

All good Bible reading must begin *inductively*; that is, the reader must come to understand the meaning of a text on its own terms, allowing the passage to speak for itself without imposing arbitrary constraints or externally devised rules. Whatever rules or constraints may apply are only those that arise from within the biblical text itself. Furthermore, the interpreter works at becoming self-aware enough to avoid being controlled by unstated or hidden agendas. And if the reader is deliberately nursing a self-conscious agenda—such as protecting the notion of a literal fulfillment of Old Testament prophecy about Israel—then that agenda must be submitted for correction (or affirmation) to the plain sense interpretation of the New Testament.

All of which leads us to the second principle accompanying the priority of inductive interpretation. This principle insists that *both testaments must be read with the same degree of literalness*. The Old Testament is not prioritized over the New, and neither is the New prioritized over the Old. Both testaments are allowed to speak for themselves, no matter how surprising or uncomfortable the plain sense meaning may prove to be. When we allow this process to unfold, we discover that there is an "intertextual" relationship between the two testaments that is seriously downplayed by Christian Zionists. Not only were the New Testament writers studying the Old Testament, but they were interpreting the Old Testament Scripture—I would say they are *reinterpreting* it—*in light of their knowledge and experience of Jesus the Messiah*. This fact is self-evident throughout the pages of the New Testament. In effect, the apostles were reading Scripture twice, as described in chapter 1. This apostolic method of interpretation should become the normative method for all Christian readers. As author Colin Chapman has written, "Christians today do not have the liberty to interpret the Old Testament in any way that appeals to them."[17] Instead, our ways of reading must become equally apostolic; at the very least, we must allow the apostolic lessons about literal Bible reading to stand as what they are—plain-sense readings of New Testament writers who are not interpreting the Old Testament literally. This principle is *not* the result of prioritizing the New Testament over the Old. It arises from simply allowing the New Testament to speak for itself after removing the muzzles of such alien

17. Chapman, *Whose Promised Land?*, 172.

presuppositions as antecedent theology and double fulfillment. New Testament creativity must be taken seriously.

A few more New Testament examples will help to illustrate these points.

"Out of Egypt I Called My Son"

In the year 722 BC the northern kingdom of Israel, sometimes called Samaria, was conquered, taken into exile, and scattered by the Assyrian Empire. During the dreadful lead-up to that catastrophe, the prophet Hosea was commissioned to urge Israel to repent of their rebelliousness if they hoped to avoid the impending storm. In Hosea chapter 11, the Lord contrasted his love and faithfulness to Israel with the people's stubborn rejection of their God. The Lord had rescued them from Egyptian slavery. Yet, they preferred false deities over their Savior. Verses 1–2 say,

> When Israel was a child, I loved him,
> and out of Egypt I called my son.
> But the more they were called,
> the more they went away from me.
> They sacrificed to the Baals
> and they burned incense to images.

There is no evidence that Hos 11:1 was ever viewed as a prophetic, messianic text prior to the writing of Matthew's Gospel. The passage does not look forward to a messiah but backward to the exodus. Hosea offered an historical reminiscence underscoring God's gracious acts of salvation during Israel's deliverance from Egyptian bondage. Yet, the Gospel of Matthew reads this Old Testament text in a curious and creative manner that was unprecedented.

Matthew 2:13–16 tells the story of King Herod's infamous "slaughter of the innocents." To evade Herod's deadly threats an angel warns Joseph to take his wife and newborn child, Jesus, into Egypt where they will find safe haven until Herod's death. Describing the family's perilous escape fleeing the land of Judah, Matthew explains, "And so was fulfilled what the Lord had said through the prophet: 'Out of Egypt I called my son'" (v. 15b). In Matthew's hands, Hosea's words no longer looked backward but forward, for the first time. In fact, Matthew's innovative reinterpretation of Hos 11:1 alters everything about the passage. Now Egypt becomes a place of safety rather than a land of bondage. God's son travels into Egypt for rescue rather than moving out of it in deliverance. The collective son, Israel, becomes the individual son, Jesus. Matthew's emphasis on that final alteration makes it clear that this pedigree of corporate sonship, from Israel to Jesus, is the reason he chose to cite this particular Old Testament text, despite the other details requiring drastic rearrangement. The association with Egypt is tangential to Matthew's main point. Jesus is revealed as the true Israel, the ultimate, beloved son of God. He is the One who will fulfill Israel's covenant responsibilities and succeed where the nation failed. All of this christological information becomes the pay dirt discovered through a plain sense interpretation of Matt 2:13–15, an unprecedented interpretation that rereads Hosea with unexpected creativity. The Old Testament was being read from back to front.

"I Will Call Them My People Who Are Not My People"

The prophet Hosea also promised the people of Israel that the Assyrian exile was not the end of their relationship with God. The Lord still had unfinished business with them. They may have turned their backs on their covenant obligations to Yahweh, but Yahweh had not turned his back completely on them. Both Hos 1:10b and 2:23 hold out the hope of future restoration:

> In the place where it was said to them, "You are not my people,"
> they will be called "children of the living God." . . .
> I will show my love to the one I called "Not my loved one."
> I will say to those called "Not my people," "You are my people."

Initially, the Lord had divorced unfaithful Israel (Hos 2:2). Their covenant had been shattered, and their intimate relationship was over. Israel was no longer God's people, no longer his beloved. Yet, the Lord could only maintain this separation for so long. Yahweh would not shun his people forever. So, eventually he relented. At some point in the future, the Lord promised to restore Israel to the intimacy of their covenant relationship. They will eventually repent of their faithlessness and come back to their God. Those who were once not his people, not his beloved, will be transformed back into his people and return as the "children of the living God."

When the apostle Paul read this prophecy, he completely redefined who were the beneficiaries of God's prevailing mercy. In Rom 9 Paul discusses the integration of Jews and gentiles as fellow members of God's new covenant in Christ. Was there some Old Testament precedent for the inclusion of uncircumcised gentiles within the covenant people alongside Jewish believers in Christ like Paul? The apostle's answer appears in Rom 9:22–26:

> What if God, although choosing to show his wrath and make his power known, bore with great patience the objects of his wrath—prepared for destruction? What if he did this to make the riches of his glory known to the objects of his mercy, whom he prepared in advance for glory—even us, whom he also called, not only from the Jews but also from the Gentiles? As he says in Hosea:
>
> "I will call them 'my people' who are not my people;
> and I will call her 'my loved one' who is not my loved one,"
>
> and,
>
> "In the very place where it was said to them,
> 'You are not my people,'
> there they will be called 'children of the living God.'"

Like Matthew, the apostle Paul offers another unprecedented reinterpretation of Hosea. Whereas the prophet had offered hope to a repentant Israel, Paul applies Hosea's words to gentiles who are joining the Christian community through faith in Christ. Originally, those who were "not my people" but then restored as "my people" were the idolatrous tribes of the Northern Kingdom. But in Romans those who are restored as God's children are transposed into formerly idolatrous gentiles who have repented and are now embraced as members of the new covenant community. Paul's reinterpretation of Hosea's original intent is so drastic and surprising that the commentator C. H. Dodd remarked, "It is rather strange that Paul has not observed that this prophecy referred to Israel."[18] Strange indeed. But the strangeness arises not from Paul's failure to grasp Hosea's message but from the apostle's commitment to rereading the Old Testament in light of its "fulfillment" in the ministry of Jesus Christ. Paul is reading the Old Testament for a second time, creatively rereading the prophet from back to front.

The plain sense of Paul's reinterpretation of Hosea makes it clear that Paul is not interpreting Hosea literally. He is interpreting Hosea christologically through the inspiration of the Holy Spirit, conforming old covenant expectations to their new covenant realization. Paul could call on the precedent of Jewish midrash as a model for his creative interpretations of Scripture. For example, the Dead Sea Scrolls reveal that the Qumran

18. Dodd, *Epistle of Paul*, 172.

community understood itself as the fulfillment of Old Testament prophecy. So, Paul is not unique in reading the prophets creatively in a "this-is-that" fashion by insisting that fulfillment has happened now.[19]

It is also worth noting that Paul never adds a proviso, as if to explain that his creative account in Romans is only the penultimate fulfillment of Hosea which still awaits the final, literal restoration of Israel at some point in the future. No. Paul offers no hint, none whatsoever, that he reads Scripture with the ostensible rules of antecedent theology or double fulfillment casting shadows from the back of his mind. Gentile membership in the community of the resurrected Jesus, on equal terms with Jewish believers, is now the literal, unexpected fulfillment of Old Testament prophecies such as Hosea's. He also holds out no hope for territorial renewal in a Jewish homeland, which certainly would have been a part of the original expectation for Hosea and his immediate audience—a repentant, restored Israel returning to its northern territory.

Neither is there any suggestion that Paul's interpretation describes only a partial or a penultimate fulfillment of Hosea's promise. There is no hint of double fulfillment; no suggestion that the era of the Christian church will be followed by a literal, landed fulfillment sometime in the future; no insinuations that Paul offers a "spiritual" interpretation now relevant for the community of Christ, but holds out a literalistic, territorial fulfillment for a certain segment of Jews in the distant future. The collective witness of the New Testament seems content to receive the Old Testament promises as richly fulfilled in Christ, in ways that were not literal, but surprising, and yet in keeping with God's faithfulness to those very promises. Paul has read Hosea backward, christologically through the lens of Christian faith under the inspiration of the Spirit of prophecy. The movement of God's grace is previewed in Yahweh's promise to reach out and restore his wayward people. God's aspirations for inclusion, for both Jews and gentiles, are foreshadowed in Hosea's words that those who were not God's people will become God's people.

19. Whether or not there remains the possibility of another future fulfillment, i.e., a double fulfillment, is not discussed. Though we may posit this as a theoretical possibility, Scripture does not answer the question. A double fulfillment remains entirely hypothetical.

"You Will Be a King's Priesthood and a Chosen Nation"

After their successful exodus from Egypt, the people of Israel were led to the foot of Mount Sinai for Yahweh's offering of the Sinai Covenant (Exod 19:5–6). This covenant was a conditional agreement introduced by an if/then clause. In other words, Yahweh promised to make Israel "a special people above all nations . . . a king's priesthood and a holy nation" if they would faithfully adhere to the Lord's covenantal demands (v. 5).

The apostle Peter looks back to the book of Exodus and rereads Sinai's if/then clause as having finally been fulfilled in the multiethnic gathering of believing Jews and gentiles. First Peter 2:9–10 cites Exod 19:5–6 and says,

> But you are a chosen people, a king's priesthood, a holy nation, a people destined for vindication, that you may declare the praises of the one who called you out of darkness into his wonderful light. Once you were not a people, but now you are the people of God; once you had not received mercy, but now you have received mercy. (My translation)

The "you" Peter is addressing are the various Christian gatherings scattered throughout Asia Minor (1 Pet 1:1). In the apostle's mind, these mixed communities, composed of Jews and gentiles together, now all compose one holy nation, one race of people, the obedient realization of God's aspirations for a compliant Israel expressed at Mount Sinai. Even though Peter never explicitly refers to these Christian bodies as the new or true or spiritual Israel, the way that they are positioned within the framework of the Sinai Covenant makes this implication clear. It also helps to explain why so many commentators who followed after Peter took that final interpretive step even though he didn't take it himself.[20]

First Peter 2:9–10 also combines the words of Exod 19 with Hos 2:23. The Hosea reference has become a familiar friend by this point in our study, and Peter is using it for exactly the same reasons the apostle Paul used it in Rom 9:24–25. Peter joins Exod 19 and Hos 2 for the same task: to demonstrate that those "who were not a people" are now transformed into "God's own people" by divine fiat, and the Old Testament's conditional promises to Israel are finally realized once and for all in the New Testament community of Christ. Once again, the Old Testament hopes for repentant Israel have been fulfilled by the new covenant people of God.

20. For a discussion of this observation, see Crump, *Like Birds in a Cage*, 115–19.

Peter's redefinition of God's covenant people is striking. Picking up the central terms for the Sinai covenant's description of Israel, Peter applies those same terms to Jews and gentiles alike in Christ. Not only are uncircumcised gentiles included within the new covenant solely on the basis of faith (remember Paul's argument in Gal 3 and Rom 4), but Jews, too, are redefined. Only now, through faith in Christ, do Jewish believers become God's "chosen people, a holy nation . . . a people called out of darkness into his wonderful light." Previously, they "were not a people, but now they are the people of God." Peter's shocking redefinition of Israel's collective identity—now centered in Christ and including uncircumcised gentiles—was a decisive one-two punch to the Jewish status quo.

It is also important to note that 1 Peter highlights the landlessness of God's new holy nation. This new covenant community is offered no hope for future real estate holdings. Rather, they are a people wandering in exile, "strangers scattered throughout the world" (1:1), "aliens" with no permanent home in this earthly terra firma (1:17; 2:11). They travel as refugees passing through a fleeting, ephemeral, earthly existence (1:3–6, 22–25 4:7; 5:1) that will never provide a physical homeland for any of God's people. Peter "never hints at holding a territorial wild card up his sleeve."[21] His teaching is clear. There is no promised land for any of God's people in the here and now. Neither is there any hint that there are two different strands of salvation-history for two different groups of people, one (the church) remaining landless while the other (the Jews) inherits the promised land. Neither Peter nor Paul gives any indication that an Old Testament written charter for promised real estate has been passed on to the New Testament era, except insofar as Christ's people will inherit the entire world at his return (Rom 4:13).

First Peter provides another plain sense example where the apostle Peter reinterprets the Old Testament through the lens of faith in Christ and his accomplishments. The salvific significance of the ancient distinction between Jews and gentiles has become irrelevant. The focus now zooms in on God's desire to forgive any and all rebellion, turning outcasts into insiders, making uncircumcised gentiles into covenant family members.

21. Crump, *Like Birds in a Cage*, 119.

Conclusion

We can see that Christian Zionists and non-Zionists operate with two different understandings of biblical authority. Zionists read the Bible as if it contained a canon within the canon; that is, as if certain Old Testament texts possess greater authority than the New Testament, especially the New Testament passages that interact with those Old Testament texts. These "premier texts" are the Old Testament prophecies that speak about the future of Israel. When understood literally this group of passages reigns supreme in the Zionist mind, taking precedence over any interpretations of these same texts offered by the New Testament authors. The rules of antecedent theology and double fulfillment act to ensure this desired result.

On the other hand, non-Zionist readings of Scripture allow both testaments to speak with the same measure of authority. There is no canon within the canon. Both the Old and the New must be read inductively, seeking to recover what the text would have meant to its original audience. What non-Zionist interpretation recognizes, however, is that when the New Testament is read inductively, we discover that the apostolic writers interpreted their Old Testament Scriptures with surprising creativity and christological inventiveness. By reading Scripture backward, from back to front through the lens of faith in Jesus, the New Testament authors teach us that the God of grace is free to fulfill his gracious promises in surprisingly effusive ways. For those who might protest, insisting that God is not allowed to reimagine the fulfillment of his promises, I can only remind them that the Lord's "judgments are unsearchable and his paths beyond tracing out" (Rom 11:33).

MYTH #3

The Israel–Palestine Conflict Is Rooted in Ancient Arab Antisemitism

LOITERING IN THE CHURCH lobby on Sunday morning is a good place for me to talk with friends about my work. Many of them know that I am a writer, so I am sometimes asked about my current project. I have learned to prepare myself for a specific set of comments whenever I am writing about Israel–Palestine. The conversations inevitably go something like this:

"David, what are you working on these days?"

"I am writing a book about Israel's war against the Palestinians."

"Good luck with that. You know it's an ancient, unending conflict. They've always hated each other, mostly because the Arabs have never accepted the Jews."

"Actually, that's not true. It's really a modern conflict. They all got along fairly well until the early twentieth century." (At this point I am often cut off.)

"But, David, it goes all the way back to Ishmael. He was the father of the Arabs, and he hated his brother Isaac. They have been fighting each other ever since."

At this point, I will attempt to catch them up on the real history of Arab–Jewish relations in Palestine—which I will do briefly in this chapter—provided they seem willing to listen. For instance, I recently met a church friend for lunch where we talked briefly about Israel's assault against Gaza. No matter how many times I tried to discuss the current political situation (and I tried to redirect his line of thinking several times), my friend's mind was stuck along one line of thought about "ancient conflicts" rooted in Gen 16:12:

> He [Ishmael] will be a wild donkey of a man;
> his hand will be against everyone
> and everyone's hand against him,
> and he will live in hostility
> towards all his brothers.

Eventually, I decided to change the subject. What makes it so difficult for my evangelical friends to see this modern conflict and all Palestinians apart from this one text in Genesis?

I'm so glad you asked.

The Role of the Scofield Reference Bible in Shaping Our (Mis)Understandings

Unfortunately, my evangelical friends find enthusiastic support for their way of seeing the contemporary situation in Israel–Palestine from American church leaders and authors who claim to speak authoritatively on this subject. For example, David Larsen, emeritus professor at Trinity Evangelical Divinity School, cavalierly declared that continuing Palestinian/Arab/Muslim (he uses the terms interchangeably) resistance to Israel's presence in the land is due to "the implacable and irrational nature of this [Muslim] hatred for everything Jewish," a hatred that has existed "from time immemorial."[1]

Similarly, best-selling evangelical author Hal Lindsey repeatedly explains throughout his book *The Everlasting Hatred: The Roots of Jihad* that Muslims "hate Jews with a visceral, bone-deep hatred that is almost impossible for the Western civilization to comprehend. In fact, this hatred goes back to the dawn of recorded history."[2] The "dawn" Lindsey refers to is "a four-thousand-year-old family feud" centered around the biblical character Ishmael; he is the supposed taproot of universal, ever-present Arab/Muslim antisemitism.[3]

These two sources are exemplary of much of the teaching that has permeated evangelical circles for decades. It makes its way into Bible studies and pulpits. No wonder my friends respond to me as they do.

One of the main roots of this line of interpretation in evangelical circles is a nineteenth-century American pastor-evangelist by the name of

1. Larsen, *Jews, Gentiles*, 164, 159; also see 153, 161, 163, 165.
2. Lindsey, *Hatred*, 2.
3. See Lindsey, *Hatred*, 14, 38, 60–64, 67–71, 86, 127.

C. I. Scofield (1843–1921). Scofield was an early advocate for an innovative version of Christian theology known as dispensationalism.[4] In 1909, Scofield published what became a very influential and broadly used study Bible using the King James Version annotated with an extensive system of footnotes. The Scofield Bible became so widely dispersed that evangelicals today can be forgiven for not realizing how idiosyncratic and novel it was in the history of biblical interpretation. Scattered throughout these notes was a running explanation of how a sequence of different "dispensations" unfolded throughout history under divine direction. A distinguishing feature of Scofield's New Testament notes was his separation of the Jewish people from the Christian church; each group has its own pathway to final salvation. The story of the church concludes with an event called the rapture, where all Christians are taken miraculously into heaven, leaving the Jews behind so that God may complete his work with them. The story of the Jews is brought to its conclusion through a seven-year period of great turmoil called the tribulation when the world pours out its antisemitic/anti-God villainy against the Jewish people gathered in the land of Israel at the battle of Armageddon. If you have attended an evangelical church for any length of time, listened to Christian radio, or watched Christian television, you are undoubtedly familiar with parts of this story.

In 1967, the editors of the Scofield Bible added a new footnote explaining the appearance of Ishmael's name in Gen 16:11: "Ishmael, the child of Sarai's and Abram's lapse into unbelief, was the progenitor of the Arabs, the traditional enemies of the Jewish people. Moreover Mohammed, the founder of Islam, whose adherents form Christianity's most difficult missionary problem, came from the line of Ishmael."[5] The note's authors made a giant, imaginative, ahistorical—one could even say mythological—leap spanning some four thousand years of history. Without a word of historical explanation, based solely on the claim in Genesis that Ishmael would "live in hostility against all his brothers," the ancient bronze age world of the biblical patriarchs is made the fountainhead from which an ostensibly universal Arab hatred of all Jews originates. If only real history writing were that simple. Real history, even when it comes to understanding the Bible, is just not that simple. We do not have the right to impose on modern history the prejudgments and prejudices that we bring to the biblical text, and

4. For a good definition, see the Wikipedia entry under "Dispensationalism."

5. Scofield, *New Scofield Reference Bible*, 25n1.

neither can we export these presuppositions back into the way we read history or look at current events.

Why did the Scofield editors feel the need to add this ahistorical note in 1967? I suspect that it was a sign of the times, so to speak. Israel's Six-Day War against its Arab neighbors, Egypt, Syria, and Jordan, erupted on June 5, 1967. Ever since Israel's declaration of independence in 1948, tensions had continually simmered between the new-born Israeli state and the surrounding Arab nations, whether in outright warfare (1948–1949) or in periodic border skirmishes. By adding this overtly racist notation to Gen 16:11,[6] labeling *all* Arabs and Muslims as "the traditional enemies of the Jewish people," the Scofield editorial committee was attempting to shed Scofield's dispensational light upon the bloody events unfolding in the modern Middle East.[7] Reading the "signs of the times" and providing a theological commentary on modern events, after all, is a typically dispensationalist thing to do.[8] In addition, I use the word "racist" here purposefully, as a way of reading that short circuits the ability to see any Palestinian or Arab as anything other than Ishmael's wild man, regardless of their religion (there are Muslim, Christian, and even Jewish Arabs) or their actual lives as teachers, laborers, parents, and children.

The Scofield Bible had sold over two million copies by the end of World War II.[9] Though definite figures are hard to find, it is not unreasonable to believe that tens of millions of copies are now circulating around the world. It's been translated into dozens of languages and the notes have been attached to a variety of translations other than the King James. The missionary zeal with which Scofield's notes have been disseminated throughout the world-wide evangelical church undoubtedly helps to explain the rapid spread of Christian Zionism throughout the Global South in countries such as Brazil, Kenya, Hong Kong, and South Korea.[10] American church historian Daniel G. Hummel has written that, "indeed,

6. Racism consists in accusing a group of people (a "race") with possessing inherent, unalterable deficiencies making them intrinsically inferior or identifiably distinct from others.

7. Despite the common confusion of Arabs and Muslims in evangelical Christian literature, the terms are not coterminous. Not all Arabs are Muslims. Just as not all Muslims are Arabs.

8. Dispensational theology has always highlighted the importance of reading the signs of the times with "a Bible in one hand and a newspaper in the other."

9. Hummel, "Bestselling Reference Bible."

10. Hummel, *Covenant Brothers*, 212–33.

the SRB's widespread adoption by lay evangelicals since 1909 has made it something of a driver of U.S. evangelical and fundamentalist culture writ large"[11]—an American culture now writ extra-large throughout the global church. Those forty-three words contained in two short sentences at the bottom of page twenty-five in the *New Scofield Reference Bible* have helped to sow the seeds of anti-Arab bigotry in evangelical fellowships around the world, propagating the naïve belief that all Arabs and Muslims inherit a nativist antisemitism—Hal Lindsey even says that it is a part of their genetic makeup![12]—which explains the periodic, hostile outbreaks between modern Israel and its Arab neighbors. Tragically, this anti-Arab racism is one of the foundation stones on which the global edifice of Christian Zionism now stands.

What Did Scofield Get Wrong About the Actual History of Middle Eastern Relations?

Avi Shlaim is a retired professor of Middle Eastern history and international relations at Oxford University. He is also a member of an academic ensemble sometimes referred to as the "new historians," a collection of Jewish-Israeli academics who dramatically overturned the traditional apple cart built by the "old historians" who long held the advantage in explaining the birth of Zionist Israel.[13] Professor Shlaim is an Arab Jew,[14] sometimes called an Oriental Jew, who was born in Baghdad, the capital of Iraq, in 1945. His recent autobiography, *Three Worlds: Memoirs of an Arab-Jew*, tells the story of his wealthy family's idyllic home life in an Arab nation, a nation where Arab Muslims, Christians, and Jews coexisted in harmony for centuries. The family's displacement from Baghdad to Israel in 1950 was forced upon them; they had no desire to leave their comfortable ancestral home or their many Muslim friends in Iraq. Their jarring relocation was forced upon them, in part, at the instigation of Israeli-Zionist agitators who carried out false flag bombing attacks in their local synagogues, shattering the peaceful environment they had always known.[15]

11. Hummel, "Bestselling Reference Bible," para. 2.

12. Lindsey, *Hatred*, 60.

13. Other new historians include Benny Morris, Ilan Pappé, and Simha Flapan.

14. This is a category of Jewish heritage that has largely been lost since the advent of Zionist Israel.

15. Shlaim, *Three Worlds*, 111–51. Shlaim describes these bombings as examples of

Shlaim's father was a successful, wealthy businessman whose family tree may have extended back as far as the Babylonian exile.[16] Neither his parents nor his grandparents had any interest in political Zionism, the European, Ashkenazi ideology that controlled the Israeli government beginning with the Israel–Arab war in 1947.[17] Zionism, born of the European pursuit of ethnic nationalism melded together with Jewish worries over European antisemitism, held "little allure" for his Middle Eastern Arab family. He explains, "We did not feel any affinity with the Zionist movement, and we experienced no inner impulse to abandon our homeland to go and live in Israel."[18] His family clung to Iraq as "the beloved homeland while the Land of Israel was a place of exile."[19] He questioned his mother about her memories of Iraq when she was ninety years old, wondering if the family had Zionist friends at the time. "No!" she replied. "Zionism is an Ashkenazi thing. It had nothing to do with us!"[20] The Shlaims regarded Israel as an extension of European colonialism; for them it was a Eurocentric state in which the older generation could never feel at home.[21]

The harmonious interreligious, multiethnic community that the Shlaim family experienced in Baghdad was not unusual for Arab Jews all throughout the Middle East at that time, including the land of Palestine.[22] While it is true that non-Muslims in the Ottoman Empire (1299–1922) periodically paid a special surtax called the *jizyah*, other discriminatory rules about how to dress and where they may be allowed to live or to build new churches or synagogues were unevenly enforced. The different non-Muslim groups were called *dhimmis* ("protected"). A system of non-Muslim

"cruel Zionism." This is not to negate the active role of the Iraq government in encouraging its Jewish population to relocate. But the Israeli authorities actively encouraged neighboring Arab governments to grow suspicious of their native Jewish citizens as potential fifth columnists acting on behalf of the new, neighboring Zionist entity.

16. Shlaim, *Three Worlds*, 8.

17. Ashkenazi Jews are of European descent, originally from central and eastern Europe. Sephardic Jews are descended from the Jewish communities driven out of Spain in the fifteenth century. Maghrebi Jews denotes those resident in North Africa. Oriental or Arab Jews described the Jewish community scattered throughout the Middle East.

18. Shlaim, *Three Worlds*, 8.

19. Shlaim, *Three Worlds*, 9.

20. Shlaim, *Three Worlds*, 9.

21. Shlaim, *Three Worlds*, 9.

22. B. Lewis, *End of Modern History*, 162, warns about two opposing mythologies. The first is a story "of a golden age of equality," while the other is about Jewish "persecution and ill treatment." He insists that "both are myths."

autonomy developed that allowed the various *dhimmis* largely to govern themselves. It was called the *millet* system; each *dhimmi* community was its own *millet* network with its own religious and political leadership. As Ottoman historian Ussama Makdisi explains, these communities "were granted religious and civil autonomy in return for their total political and fiscal subordination."[23] The empire was vast and the circumstances of individual *millets* could vary from region to region.[24] But peaceful coexistence was the norm in an empire-wide system of confraternity that Professor Makdisi calls the "ecumenical frame."

The Ottoman social structures securing this ecumenical frame were secured even more broadly with two mid-nineteenth-century imperial proclamations. These two proclamations initiated a period known as the *Tanzimat*, the reordering of the empire.[25] The first proclamation was the 1839 declaration of nondiscrimination between Muslim and non-Muslim subjects; the second appeared in the imperial constitution of 1876 guaranteeing equal citizenship for all Ottoman subjects.[26] Historian Michelle U. Campos describes the 1876 constitution as the Ottoman Magna Carta.[27] This ethos of interreligious fraternity and shared citizenship persisted for decades throughout the Arab world after the dissolution of the empire. Its tragic erosion in the land of Palestine began in the late nineteenth–early twentieth centuries with the immigration of European Ashkenazi Jews wedded to the ideology known as political Zionism.[28]

The Collision of Cultures That Changed the Middle East

Of course, not all Jewish immigrants from Europe were Zionist partisans—in fact, Zionists were a minority—just as only a minority of these emigrants

23. Makdisi, *Age of Coexistence*, 30; also B. Lewis, *Jews of Islam*, 45.

24. See B. Lewis, *Jews of Islam*, 31. Lewis observes that "on the whole one gets the impression that they (the non-fiscal regulations marking non-Muslim identity) were more often disregarded than strictly enforced." Also see B. Lewis, *Semites and Anti-Semites*, 122–23.

25. Campos, *Ottoman Brothers*, 23.

26. Makdisi, *Age of Coexistence*, 10.

27. Campos, *Ottoman Brothers*, 24; also see 65.

28. Bernard Lewis, respected authority on Middle Eastern history, writes in *Semites and Anti-Semites*, 117, "For most of the fourteen hundred years or so of the Arab Jewish encounter, the Arabs have not in fact been anti-Semitic as that word is used in the West."

fled to Palestine. The majority immigrated to the Americas. But those Jewish Zionists who did migrate to the strip of Middle Eastern territory hugging the southeast coast of the eastern Mediterranean were entering an Arab society that they knew little if anything about, creating an environment ripe for consistent, serious misunderstanding. As we have seen, Palestine had a long history of religious coexistence where an "Arab" could be a Muslim, a Christian, or a Jew. The so-called Jewish problem—that is, answering the question of what to do with Jewish residents in a European continent that was rapidly building state identities around ethnic nationalist divisions—was a strictly European issue with no parallel in the Arab world. The Middle East had no "Jewish problem." Neither were there Arab parallels to the type of European antisemitism that had generated multiple pogroms, periodic persecutions, and wholesale expulsions of Jews from their traditional homes.[29]

Consequently, when the inevitable Arab opposition to political Zionism finally arose, the circumstances were interpreted from two opposing vantage points. These different perspectives produced irreconcilable differences that were sharpened by three pivotal events. The first was the publication of the Balfour Declaration (November 1917) in which Great Britain promised to encourage "the establishment in Palestine of a national home for the Jewish people"; the second was the dissolution of the Ottoman Empire at the end of World War I (1918), which was then divided between the colonial powers, France and Great Britain; the third event was the inclusion of the Balfour Declaration within the mandatory responsibilities regarding the governing of Palestine handed over to Great Britain by the League of Nations (1922). All three of these events highlighted the fact that the land of Palestine was to remain a pawn on the chess board of European colonial power, and those powers, chiefly Great Britain, would do with her as they wished. By the 1920s, it was impossible for the Arab population of Palestine—Muslim, Christian, and native Jews alike—not to view political Zionism as another extension of European imperialism imposing yet another colonial project upon them without their consent.[30]

Whether from ignorance, arrogance, desperation, or a combination of all three, most Zionist settlers/colonizers could never understand their

29. B. Lewis, *Jews of Islam*, 185, explains the well-established position in Ottoman studies that the earliest antisemitic literature in Arabic was translated from French toward the end of the nineteenth century in connection with the Dreyfus controversy. Again, there was no "ancient hatred."

30. See Said, *Question of Palestine*.

situation from the Arab point of view.[31] Instead, they could only see their uncomfortable encounters with antagonistic Arabs through European eyes. From the mistaken perspective of political Zionism, the brand of virulent antisemitism they had known in Europe was a universal, gentile problem and was as deeply rooted in the former Ottoman Empire as it was anywhere else. From this erroneous Zionist perspective, Arab natives resented Jewish settlement because the Arabs were antisemites, hostile to all Jews. However, from the Arab/Palestinian perspective, this influx of European Ashkenazi settlers represented a rapacious British empire gobbling up more Arab land for another British colony. These two opposing worldviews would forever remain at loggerheads.

While this is not the story told by Zionists today, whether Jewish or Christian, it is the story uncovered, documented, and propagated by contemporary historians of the Ottoman Empire. For instance, Michelle U. Campos, professor of Jewish studies and history at the University of Pennsylvania and author of *Ottoman Brothers: Muslims, Christians, and Jews in Early Twentieth-Century Palestine*, explains how Jewish immigrants did not meet a native people innately prejudiced against Jews. Rather, the alienation between the two groups

> occurred hand in hand with the growth of the Zionist movement, which itself actively sought to segregate indigenous Jews from their neighbors, their environment, and their empire. Ultimately, though, separation in Palestine between Jews and Arabs came about as the *result* of the Zionist-Palestinian conflict—it was not the cause.[32]

There were also numerous peaceful civil actions taken by Arab leaders to combat the Zionist efforts at religious-national separation and to stop the march of Zionist settler-colonialism. Widespread violence was *not* the first option selected for Arab resistance. For example, both Muslim and Christian newspapers worked hard to educate the Palestinian public, warning about the obvious long-term goals of Zionist immigration: an exclusively

31. There were a few exceptions such as the early immigrant Ahad Ha'am. Ha'am was disgusted by the regular abuse heaped upon the indigenous Arabs by Ashkenazi settlers. He wrote that "if Palestinian Jewry is unable to exercise restraint and decency now that it holds little power, how much worse will it be when we control the land and its Arab inhabitants?" Quoted in Makdisi, *Age of Coexistence*, 165–66.

32. Campos, *Ottoman Brothers*, 19.

Jewish national homeland in Palestine.[33] Since the Zionist community had political representation in the various offices of the British Mandate, Palestinian Arabs formed their own political bodies to peacefully seek a mutually acceptable alternative. The First Muslim–Christian Congress convened in Jerusalem in 1919, reflecting the nascent nationalism stirred by colonial Zionism and seeking possible methods of confronting the colonial threat. Muslim and Christian Arabs worked closely together to form the Syro–Palestinian Congress in Geneva in 1921 to protest the British Mandate. The First Congress of Arab Students formed in Jaffa in 1929 where secondary-school students read nationalist poetry and criticized both the British Mandate as well as the Arab leaders they saw as collaborationists working against Palestinian interests. The General Islamic Congress was formed in Jerusalem in 1931 calling for an international boycott of all Zionist products. The Nablus Arab Patriotic Society organized the Nablus Congress in 1931 modeling itself along the lines of "Gandhian anticolonial civil disobedience" and called for a general strike in protest of the Mandate's arming of Zionist settlements.[34] In 1939 the Arab Office, an organization formed to lobby against Zionism in Western capitals, proposed the creation of an ecumenical, multireligious state advocating, in effect, for the resurrection of a superior form of *Tanzimat* in Palestine (see above). Its chief advocate, Albert Hourani, proposed the creation of a "self-governing state, with its Arab majority, but with full rights for the Jewish citizens of Palestine . . . [including] full civil and political rights, control over their own communal affairs and municipal autonomy."[35] In effect, Arab leaders were proposing something with which their forefathers had long experience—the continuation of the confraternity, ethnic and religious coexistence that the Ottomans had provided the Muslim, Christian, and Jewish members of the Arab world for centuries. Viewing such proposals of ecumenical equality through European, Ashkenazi eyes, Zionists only remained fearful over their minority status in an overwhelmingly Arab land. Political Zionists remained entrenched in their demands for a majority-Jewish nation-state founded upon as much Palestinian land as possible denuded of as many Palestinians as possible.

33. See Campos, *Ottoman Brothers*, 133–65.

34. Makdisi, *Age of Coexistence*, 182; the truncated, condensed history of events listed in this paragraph is constructed from pp. 166–84.

35. Makdisi, *Age of Coexistence*, 187; for further discussion of Arab-Jewish coexistence in the land of Palestine, see Jacobson and Naor, *Oriental Neighbors*; Robinson, *Citizen Strangers*.

Orientalism and Anti-Arab Racism Today

In an ideal world, people who say they follow Jesus would be the first to identify disparaging, racist language; the first to condemn it; and the first to abandon it, consigning it to the dustbin of history. One would have hoped, for example, that Hal Lindsey's adamant promotion of racist stereotypes about *all* Arabs possessing an inherent, unalterable hatred of *all* Jews throughout *all* of history would have made it difficult, if not impossible, to find an audience with Christian readers.[36] But such is not the case, at least in part, because Christian Zionism, by way of its long-term connection with dispensational theology and its distorted (mis)understanding of Palestinian history, is not only intertwined with anti-Arab racism (see above) but is made sympathetic to a mode of thinking about the Arab world called Orientalism.[37]

Racism imaginatively gathers an entire class of people[38]—identifiable by distinctive markers such as skin color, language, place of origin, etc.—and labels them all as possessing the same unchangeable, negative characteristics. Their "racial" deficiencies are uniform, inherent, hereditary, and unalterable. These unalterable deficiencies become the root cause of their supposed inferiority. Fortunately, the days are long past when a person could openly exclaim in polite society that all X are lazy; all X are drunkards; all X are dim-witted. (Although many would claim that this anti-racist advance is being rolled back in America today.)

Unfortunately, in Western society, racial stereotypes about Arabs and other Eastern/Asian people groups remain acceptable.[39] The semi-automatic association of the word "terrorist" with "Arab" or "Muslim" is a predictable connection in Western society. Columbia professor of comparative literature Edward Said (deceased) wrote the groundbreaking book on this subject in 1978 titled *Orientalism*; it was followed by his equally important book *Covering Islam: How the Media and the Experts Determine How We*

36. See his best-selling book *The Everlasting Hatred* published by WND Books.

37. For a discussion of the latently racist undertones in dispensational Bible reading, see Crump, "Echoes of Slavery," and "Christian Zionist Bible Reading."

38. The word itself testifies to the way linguistic conventions can fossilize and fall out of step with evolving social norms. Today it is generally understood that there is only one human race. Yet, the word "racism," derived from the past belief in multiple races of humanity, persists in describing discrimination between different types of people.

39. "Malicious generalizations about Islam have become the last acceptable form of denigration of foreign culture in the West"; see Said, *Covering Islam*, xii.

See the Rest of the World. According to Said, the story of Orientalism begins with European colonialism, the British Empire and Western expansion into "the Orient," including India, South Asia, East Asia, and the Middle East. Early European and British explorers, scientists, academics, travel writers, and leaders of the many military campaigns pursuing territorial conquest all launched a new genre of politicized literature describing the exotic, mysterious Orient to Western readers. They spoke in sweeping generalities, painting with broad brushstrokes for a white audience that considered itself to be exceptional and superior—after all, they were the civilized explorers now cataloguing the new types of humanity being uncovered. These broad brushstrokes romanticized the Oriental as ancient, primitive, unchanging, mysterious, violent, libidinous, and inscrutable. The methods of Orientalist scholarship transformed the people of the Orient into "the Other," strangers par excellence open to Western scrutiny if not to understanding. Said summarizes Orientalism by saying,

> It is therefore correct that every European in what he could say about the Orient, was consequently a racist, an imperialist, and almost totally ethnocentric. . . . [H]uman societies, at least the more advanced cultures, have rarely offered the individual anything but imperialism, racism, and ethnocentrism for dealing with "other" cultures. . . . My contention is that Orientalism is fundamentally a political doctrine willed over the Orient because the Orient was weaker than the West, which [combined] the Orient's difference with its weakness.[40]

The nineteenth-century Ashkenazi leaders of political Zionism deeply imbibed European Orientalism for themselves in the form of anti-Arab racism. It is easier to subjugate and expel a group of people when the conquerors view the natives as inferiors. In this way, the power of European, Ashkenazi whiteness predetermined the Zionist attitude toward Palestinian Arabs in the same way that American white supremacy stripped black African slaves of their humanity. Numerous examples could be cited to illustrate this point. Chaim Weizmann was the chief Zionist representative to the British government when in 1918 he commented to Lord Balfour (author of the Balfour Declaration) on "the treacherous nature of the Arab, who screams as often as he can and blackmails as much as he can."[41] Weiz-

40. Said, *Orientalism*, 204.

41. Quoted in Makdisi, *Age of Coexistence*, 167. Note that Balfour ignores the fact that the Arab may well be "screaming" over the Zionist appropriation of their land.

mann consistently opposed all suggestions of a binational or multiethnic state because "democracy was not appropriate for a backward peoples," a people "too primitive" to grasp civil governance.[42] Ze'ev Jabotinsky, the leader of Revisionist Zionism, loudly condemned any attempt to give Arabs a voice in the future of Palestine. He saw "the Arabs as a 'primitive', 'arrogant' race which was 'contemptible and repellent.'"[43] The British Palin Commission released its study on the causes of Palestinian Arab unrest in 1920. Contrasting the Muslim and Jewish communities, the report explained how the timid Arab peasant was "apathetic and slow in his intelligence (as compared to) the vigorous mental force of the Jew."[44] Such denigrating descriptions have persisted into the modern period. Israeli Prime Minister Menachem Begin described Palestinians as "grasshoppers" and "two-footed beasts." Benjamin Netanyahu has accused Palestinians of being "wild beasts" and "predators."[45] Israeli Defense Minister Yoav Gallant justified Israel's call for "a complete siege" against Gaza by describing Palestinians as "human animals."[46] I could continue with many more anti-Arab racist quotations, all of them undergirded by the Orientalist ideology widely disseminated by the educated class of Western Orientalists and adopted by Ashkenazi Zionists. Hal Lindsey's racist comments about the implacable hatreds of wild Arabs are completely at home with the Orientalist bigotry of modern Zionism.

One of the more blatant, contemporary examples of Orientalist anti-Arab racism appeared in some news reports contrasting the war in Ukraine with Israel's assault on Gaza. Western broadcasters reminded viewers that Ukraine is "European," "white," "Christian," and "civilized." Ukrainian refugees are "like us." They didn't look like your "typical refugees" because they were "relatively prosperous, well-dressed and middle-class." The Orientalist *bona fides* of multiple broadcasters appeared prominently, however, when their compiled news reports all describe brown-skinned Palestinian refugees as "the Other." These Palestinians were nothing at all like us but were

42. Quoted in Flapan, *Zionism and the Palestinians*, 71.

43. Quoted in Flapan, *Zionism and the Palestinians*, 115.

44. Quoted in Makdisi, *Age of Coexistence*, 176.

45. For a long list of examples where Israeli leaders use degrading animalistic metaphors to describe Palestinians, see Wikipedia, "Animal Stereotypes of Palestinians."

46. Al Jazeera, "Israeli Defense Minister Orders."

representative of undeveloped "third-world nations" that, by implication, were dominated by chaos, strife, and instinctive sectarianism.[47]

The Orientalist ethos of Western colonialism remains deeply embedded within the Zionist psyche wherever it appears, whether in Israel or in Christian Zionist congregations around the world.[48] But given the insistence of Zionist apologists on describing Israel as an exclusively *Jewish* state offering a homeland to all the Jews of the world, it is not hard to understand why people in the Arab street would eventually confuse Israeli behavior with a universal Jewish culpability. In this way, Zionist colonial, expansionist rhetoric about a primarily Jewish greater Israel potentially offering refuge to all the world's Jews, thus tying Israel to world Jewry, may encourage Middle Eastern antisemitism.[49] Yet, as I have shown, Arab antisemitism has never been hereditary, inevitable, or universal. Some years ago, I had an American Jewish acquaintance who was living in a Palestinian refugee camp in the West Bank. He had begun a business with a Palestinian partner, and the two of them traveled extensively throughout the Middle East. I once asked him if he ever experienced anything resembling antisemitism either in his travels or in the refugee camp he called home. He answered by saying, "No. Not once." Granted, this is anecdotal evidence. But it only takes a handful of anecdotes to puncture the validity of a racist stereotype.

Conclusion

Though I am not Jewish, I can say that in all my years of visiting Palestine and living in a Palestinian community, I have never heard an antisemitic remark, much less a hateful tirade.[50] It is long past time for political Zionism to confess its own role in creating interracial strife in Israel–Palestine.

47. Watch the YouTube video compilation of reports in NowThis Impact, "Hypocritical Media Coverage of Ukraine vs. the Middle East."

48. Examining the profound irony of Christians in the Global South adhering to Orientalist anti-Arab racism, viz. their Christian Zionist ideology, would require an additional chapter of its own.

49. B. Lewis, *Semites and Anti-Semites*, 255, also recognizes this problem, labeling it antisemitism. He says, "For the anti-Semite, all Jews are Zionists and all are pro-Israel, since Jew, Zionist, and Israeli are interchangeable terms." Yet, he fails to recognize the pivotal role of Zionist rhetoric in facilitating this popular confusion.

50. Admittedly, this could be due to some rule about Palestinian courtesy with guests. But the fact remains: though I have heard many criticisms of Israel and Zionism—criticisms that I share—I have never heard a racist, antisemitic remark.

It is also long past time for Christian Zionists everywhere to renounce their affinity with Zionist racism in order more vigorously to express their Christian allegiance to Jesus Christ. Ishmael the wild man is not the prototype for Palestinian relations with Zionist Israel today. Nor is blessed Isaac the archetype for God's attitude toward the modern Israeli state. All Christians must view Palestinians and Israelis alike as fellow human beings, equally loved by God, held to the same standards of justice and mercy. In today's circumstances where the modern political conflict continues, Israel remains the dominant oppressor, slaughtering innocent Palestinians. It is only right that the followers of Jesus call for an end to all violence, condemn Israel's war crimes, and demand that Western governments withdraw their support for the Zionist nation-state.

No, the modern hostilities between Israelis and Palestinians have not existed "from time immemorial"; nor do their mythological origins appear in the Old Testament stories about Hagar and her "wild man" of a son, Ishmael. The origins of this simmering conflict are much more prosaic and historically plausible. They began with a British enterprise to colonize Palestine with Jews drawn primarily from eastern and central Europe. When these two different people groups met, European Jews and Palestinian Arabs, each knowing little if anything about the other's history or culture, the situation was ripe for serious, deep-seated misunderstanding.

MYTH #4

Israel's Victory over the Arab States in 1948 Was a Miracle

I THOUGHT THAT MY presentation describing Palestinian life in the occupied territory of the West Bank had gone well. Many people thanked me for opening their eyes and shedding new light onto issues they had previously known nothing about. A few people had become upset and voiced their disagreements (some quite loudly), but that was to be expected in any conversation about Israel–Palestine, not least with evangelical churchgoers.

Most of the crowd had already left the church auditorium as I finally began to make my way toward the exit. I was intercepted by an elderly gentleman who hurriedly approached me wide-eyed and agitated. As I said hello and shook his hand, he blurted out this question, "So, you don't believe that Israel's victory in 1948 was a miracle of God?"

"No, I don't," I said.

His facial expression shifted from shocked to dumbfounded as he swiftly turned and walked away before I could say anything more. I was happy to explain myself further, but obviously I had said everything he believed he needed to hear. I suspect he had concluded that I did not believe in the authority of Scripture, nor that God can work in human history.

For many Christian Zionists, believing that Israel's victory in the Palestine war of 1947–1949 was obtained by divine miracle is essential to any reasonable belief in biblical authority and the sovereignty of God. The logic of the argument works like this: (1) the Old Testament predicted that God will someday reestablish the nation of Israel in the promised land (see chapters 1 and 2); (2) in the Palestine war the tiny, fledgling state of Israel fought against overwhelming odds as the collective armies of five Arab states amassed to wipe Israel off the map; (3) just as the biblical David could only defeat the Philistine giant Goliath by divine intervention, so Israel's victory over the Arabs must also be seen as a miracle of God; (4) therefore, Israel's miraculous military victory must be understood as the fulfillment of biblical prophecy, an example of God's faithfulness demonstrated in human history, and thus tangible evidence for the trustworthiness of holy Scripture.

There is no need, however, to accept either the purported logic of this argument or the assumed connection between its conclusion and a belief in biblical authority. Many Christians believe as I do that God works in history and that all Scripture is divinely inspired but do not feel that these statements of faith inevitably lead to any particular understanding about the outcome of the Palestine war in 1947–1949. The biblical basis for separating those two positions has already been laid out in chapters 1 and 2 of this book. By not accepting the argument's premise (that God promises the literal restoration of physical Israel in the promised land), there is no need to interpret any of Israel's military successes, whether in 1948 or 1967 (when Israel captured the West Bank from Jordan), or even now as Israel unleashes genocide on Gaza, as acts of God fulfilling biblical prophecy.

More than that, many Israeli historians now argue that Israel was not a tiny, unprepared nation vastly outnumbered by five, large, well-equipped Arab armies.[1] In fact, as numerous international observers pointed out at the time, Israel was in a far stronger position than any of its Arab opponents. A British high official in the Mandatory Government (on March 3, 1948) stated that "he couldn't understand how anybody could attach any serious importance to the Arab stories" about their superior military might. Furthermore, "he was quite convinced that the Jews could well hold their own against an Arab attack."[2] Based on the best sources and analysis, Israel's victory was one of superior might facilitated by the British army and was all but a foregone conclusion.

Conflicting Objectives and Dueling Narratives

The fact that many of Israel's contemporary supporters remain unaware of this newer, more thoroughly documented historical narrative is testimony

1. See Pappé, *Making*.

2. Flapan, *Birth of Israel*, 191; for a lengthy list of the international officials and their observations on Israeli military superiority, see 190–92.

to the effectiveness of Israel's foundational, nationalistic propaganda campaign. To call the traditional storyline of Israel's successful rise as a Jewish nation-state propaganda is not to dismiss it as somehow uniquely malicious. Every nation constructs its own nationalistic origin-story designed to inculcate patriotic devotion among its citizens, citizens who will then volunteer for public service, make sacrifices for the national interest, answer the call for military enlistment, and gladly lay down their lives for their beloved country. It is no secret that the creation of the US public education system in the nineteenth century was motivated in part by a similar desire to cultivate and nourish young American patriots.

Professor Benny Morris is a leading Israeli historian who distinguishes between two schools of Israeli history. The first, he explains, are "the old historians, who perhaps should more accurately be called chroniclers, [who] offered a simplistic and consciously pro-Israeli interpretation of the past and generally avoided mention of anything that reflected poorly upon Israel."[3] For the old historians, telling the truth about Israel's history generally took a back seat to bolstering what they perceived as Israel's patriotic national interests.[4] In other words, the older history served the purpose of nationalistic apologetics, portraying and defending a story of Israel's origins that buttressed the state's interests in nurturing devout patriots. Consequently, the "purest expression" of the old history, according to Morris, is found in Israeli schoolbooks.[5]

The second group of Israeli historians are those Professor Morris refers to as "the new historians" (including himself) who have rewritten Israel's history books by both "looking afresh" at the historical record as well as by examining for the first time official state documents declassified in the 1980s.[6] Those declassifications made available an avalanche of government papers that were inaccessible to the earlier generation of historians. Furthermore, focusing on the period of 1947–1951, Morris insists that "the new generation of Israeli historians have been capable of at least a measure of impartiality."[7] Because the new historians are not veterans of the Palestine war, their personal interests, memories, and emotional lives are not so

3. Morris, "New Historiography," 5.

4. Morris, "New Historiography," 4, 6.

5. Morris, "New Historiography," 5. David Ben-Gurion was Israel's first prime minister, the national equivalent of America's George Washington.

6. Morris, "New Historiography," 6–7.

7. Morris, "New Historiography," 7.

closely tied to the histories they write about the events of 1947–1949. As a result of these two factors, "a more accurate and realistic understanding of the roots of the Israeli–Arab conflict is now emerging."[8] There can be no doubt that the new historians have provided a more accurate, less propagandistic picture of Israel's origin story, warts and all.

However, not everyone accepts the findings of the new historians, as we will see. Some continue to cling to the older storylines and to place their faith in the myth of a tiny, fragile Israel nearly overwhelmed by a huge hive of Arab hornets. But they can do this only by ignoring, suppressing, or confusing the abundant evidence now on offer from the new historians.[9] Yes, history writing involves interpretation, and not everyone will interpret events in the same way. But every valid interpretation will take account of all the available facts. Even in this era of moral relativism, facts matter. They cannot be ignored, certainly not by Christian people, or any person of integrity who claims to value the truth.

Retelling the Old, Fallacious Propaganda Story

David Brog is a contemporary, Jewish Zionist author who largely ignores the hard-hitting historical work of the new historians in favor of the patriotic glamor of the old. Brog is the former executive director of pastor John Hagee's organization, Christians United for Israel (CUFI), the largest Christian Zionist organization in the country.[10] He is now the head of the Maccabee Task Force, an organization focused on combatting the global Boycott, Divestment and Sanctions (BDS) campaign seeking to impose economic sanctions against Israel. A self-described "champion of Israel," Brog also happens to be the cousin of the former Israeli Prime Minister Ehud Barak and is author of the book *Standing with Israel: Why Christians Support Israel*, a popular title among Christian Zionists.

It is not surprising then that Brog, committed as he is to defending political Zionism and the Jewish state, continues to parley in the traditional Israeli national mythology constructed by the old historians, among the most aggressive propagandists for Israel. In 2018 he published *Reclaiming*

8. Morris, "New Historiography," 27.

9. This is why the Israeli government has reclassified many of these documents so that they are no longer available to historians and other researchers.

10. For a succinct biography of Brog, see the *Forward* article, Kornbluh, "He Was the Head."

Israel's History: Roots, Rights, and the Struggle for Peace, in which he repeats the mythological view of the origins of the Israeli state. After cataloguing the five Arab states (Egypt, Jordan, Syria, Iraq, and Lebanon) that fought against Israel in 1948, Brog begins his discussion of the Palestine war by saying, "Suddenly, the tiny and pathetically equipped Jewish army faced a war on multiple fronts against armies far larger, better armed, and better trained than their own."[11] Brog's declaration, however, about the "tiny" Jewish state is not so much a reclaiming of history as it is a recycling of the antiquated propaganda about Israel's miraculous national origins. For the historical evidence does not support Brog's retelling no matter the number of Israeli apologists and Christian Zionists who would applaud his assertiveness. Every claim Brog makes has been proven wrong through the documents uncovered by the new historians.

The Truth About the 1947–1949 War

There are two principal errors in the way the old historians, and now their younger popularizers, continue to describe the Palestine war: first, the Israeli forces were perennially weaker, smaller, and "pathetically equipped"; second, the Arab armies were larger, better armed and better equipped. In fact, just the opposite was the case.

The Palestine war is commonly divided into two phases: the Civil War, which lasted from November 29, 1947, to May 14, 1948; and the Arab War, which began on May 15, 1948, and ended tentatively with the beginning of armistice negotiations between Israel and the individual Arab states (finalized between February and July 1949).

The Civil War was sparked by the United Nations' approval of its Partition Resolution 181 intended to divide Palestine into two states, one for the Palestinians and another for the Jews, with Jerusalem under international control. Unsurprisingly, UN approval of a plan to give a large portion of the Palestinian homeland over to a Jewish nation-state—to be colonized by recent European immigrants—caused an uproar throughout the indigenous, Palestinian population. The second phase of the Arab War broke out when Britain's United Nations Mandate over Palestine came to an end, and Great Britain began to withdraw both its troops and civil administration from the region. This British withdrawal, combined with the Zionist government's declaration of independence on May 15, 1948, triggered a military attack

11. Brog, *Reclaiming*, 10.

by five neighboring Arab states.[12] Rather than allow Palestine to become the property of a Zionist nation-state, Palestine's Arab neighbors saw an opportunity to invade for their own individual nationalistic purposes.

It is important to keep these two phases of the Palestine war in mind. The war had been unfolding for five and a half months before any Arab army sent its troops into Palestine. Prior to that moment the fighting occurred between local, Palestinian village militias and the Jewish military forces that would eventually merge to become the Israel Defense Forces (IDF). Unlike the Zionists, however, the Palestinians had never been allowed, by either the British or the Ottomans, to build a national military organization.[13] Their local militias were poorly armed and generally disorganized, rarely working together.[14] In the words of the new historian Ilan Pappé, these groups "refused to coordinate their activities with the local leadership and in some cases even deserted the battlefield at the crucial moment."[15] Though ambushes and counterattacks against civilians occurred on both sides, Sir Alan Cunningham, British high commissioner at the time, said that the Palestinians' primary weapons were "sticks and stones." According to Cunningham, it was the Zionist settlers who escalated the level of violence, while "the Arab Higher Committee as a whole, and the Mufti in particular, wanted non-violent resistance—boycott—and were not in favour of serious outbreaks." British officers reported numerous cases of Palestinian village leaders visiting adjacent Jewish settlements to say that "they wanted to remain on friendly terms with their Jewish neighbors."[16] Ironically, in his attempt to undermine the concept of Palestinian nationalism as a motivating factor in unifying Palestinians in 1948, even Brog admits that "only a small minority of Palestine's Arabs volunteered to fight the Jews." Those who did step forward fought through a multitude of local militias which aimed to drive the Zionist militias "from their particular towns and neighborhoods. But only in 'extremely rare' cases did these fighters venture beyond their immediate environs."[17] Furthermore, as Brog also admits, few

12. The British authorities had allowed the Zionists to construct the basic bureaucracy of a nascent state during the Mandate period beginning in 1922. No such liberties were allowed the Palestinians.

13. Morris, *Righteous Victims*, 194–95.

14. Morris, *Righteous Victims*, 195.

15. Pappé, *Making*, 65.

16. Suarez, *State of Terror*, 241.

17. Brog, *Reclaiming*, 49.

if any of the villages located in the territory that would eventually be known as the West Bank participated in the fighting.[18]

We see that the old history's portrayal of a uniform Palestinian explosion of anti-Jewish violence is completely unfounded. The Palestinian response to the UN Partition vote also included numerous, large-scale peaceful demonstrations denouncing the UN decision. On December 5, over thirteen hundred Palestinians in Gaza conducted an orderly march with banners saying, "Down with Truman and Down with Partition." Three to four thousand Palestinians peacefully demonstrated for four hours near Khan Yunis and then sent a delegation to express their dissent to local police. Near Kefar Saba, one thousand marched in another peaceful protest against Partition. British security forces reported that "the Arabs as a whole are loath to start hostilities."[19] Benny Morris offers numerous examples testifying to the pacific inclinations of Palestinian villagers. He says, "During the war's first three months [December 1947 to February 1948], more than two dozen Arab villages and tribes sent out feelers to Jewish officials to conclude local non-belligerency agreements. They were mainly motivated by fear of Jewish attack or reprisals."[20] Morris notes "the Arab [i.e., Palestinian] public's reluctance to fight." He cites a Hagana (the Yishuv's official military wing) intelligence report saying that "most of the [Palestinian] public will be willing to accept partition" and that the villagers of Galilee "lacked any desire to get involved in a war with the Jews."[21] We see that the Palestinian population was far more diverse and generally inclined toward a peaceful resolution than the old historians were ever willing to admit.

Furthermore, the Zionist community (typically referred to as the Yishuv) had spent years preparing for war against the Palestinian villages scattered throughout the countryside. The Jewish Agency[22] was conducting a war-planning program called the Village Files which dispersed numerous surveillance teams, groups that disguised themselves as "hiking parties," throughout Palestine.[23] In addition to extensive mapping and photographic

18. Brog, *Reclaiming*, 130.

19. Suarez, *State of Terror*, 241.

20. Morris, *Birth*, 92.

21. Morris, *Birth*, 87.

22. Established in 1929, the Jewish Agency works in coordination with the World Zionist Organization to promote and secure the national interests of the state of Israel.

23. On the manufacture and use of the Village Files, see Pappé, *Ethnic Cleansing*, 17–22.

operations, these "hikers" collected detailed demographic information on every community, no matter how small, collating everything needed "to determine how best to attack the villages," as one hiker put it.[24] This information also enabled the Hagana (the official Zionist military organization, later to become the IDF) "to conduct more accurate simulated assaults" against "dummy" villages, built to resemble actual villages, while the regular "hikes" camouflaged the military personnel moving to and from hidden military training settlements.[25] When the Civil War finally broke out in 1947, the well-prepared Zionist forces were more than ready to overwhelm the disconnected Palestinian villages with their individual neighborhood defense squads. Before the war was over, more than four hundred of these villages would be overrun and erased from the map.[26]

At this point, I should not neglect to mention that this early phase of the war also marked the beginning of the Palestinian refugee crisis, which eventually engulfed at least 750,000 people. The mythological origin story of Israel usually makes two points with respect to these war refugees. David Brog repeats them both, absolving Israel of any responsibility and placing all the blame for the refugee crisis squarely on the backs of the Arab states that attacked Israel. He says, first, that the refugees "fled because they were ordered to do so by certain Arab leaders and commanders."[27] And second, Brog claims that "the Arab states did not invade Israel to help the Palestinian refugees. It was the Arab invasion that *produced* the Palestinian refugees" (his emphasis).[28] However, the new historians have shown that both claims are false. Professor Morris has studied this piece of Palestinian history most intensively. He reaches two important conclusions: first, his book *The Birth of the Palestinian Refugee Problem Revisited* catalogues the many occasions where thousands of refugees were forced to flee their homes during the Civil War phase of the conflict, long before any of the Arab states sent troops into Palestine; and second, at the end of his exhaustive study, after combing through the archives and listening to many hours of radio broadcast recordings, Morris finally concluded, "I have found no evidence to show that the AHC [the Arab Higher Committee] or the Arab

24. Suarez, *State of Terror*, 88.
25. Suarez, *State of Terror*, 88.
26. See W. Khalidi, *All That Remains.*
27. Brog, *Reclaiming*, 10.
28. Brog, *Reclaiming*, 11.

leaders outside Palestine issued blanket instructions, by radio or otherwise, to the [Palestinian] inhabitants to flee."[29]

Who Outnumbered Who?

We have seen that writers such as Brog, who continue to trade in the antiquated old history, insist that Israel was outmanned and outgunned during the war.[30] While it is true that Jewish weaponry, munitions, and equipment were stretched very thin during the early stages of the Civil War, this paucity of armaments began to change dramatically in late April–early May 1948. Although Great Britain and the United States had imposed a trade embargo prohibiting the sale of any war matériel to either side in the conflict, the Soviet Union, via its satellite state Czechoslovakia, broke with the blockade and began transporting large caches of weapons and equipment to the Jewish military.[31] This transfer of war matériel increased significantly throughout the first truce, from June 11 through July 8, 1948, and continued beyond, well into the Arab War beginning on May 15.[32] Once this underground transfer of arms from Eastern Europe had begun, Zionist forces would never again be poorly equipped, as Israel's ability to manufacture its weaponry domestically also continued to expand. To quote Ilan Pappé, history professor at the College of Social Sciences and International Studies at the University of Exeter, "the military balance tipped in favour of the Jews during the truce" (a supply program which also violated that truce).[33] The Arab states, on the other hand, never benefited from a similar weapons pipeline; the trade blockade remained firmly enforced against weapons and equipment being transferred to the Arab states. Great Britain even refused to trade with the British-led Arab Legion of Jordan.[34]

The mythology about the overwhelming size of the Arab armies is rooted in a logical mistake which assumes that the size of an army is relative to the size of the nation. That is, Israel was small (650,000 Jews) when compared to the much larger Arab population living in the five invading Arab countries (approximately forty million people). The Palestinian population

29. Morris, *Birth*, 594.

30. Brog, *Reclaiming*, 10–11.

31. Morris, *Righteous Victims*, 193; Pappé, *Making*, 142–43.

32. Pappé, *Making*, 142.

33. Pappé, *Making*, 143.

34. Pappé, *Making*, 111, 142.

alone (1.2 million) enjoyed a roughly two-to-one population advantage.[35] Therefore, because of these demographic disparities, the five Arab armies must have been significantly larger than Israel's.[36] But there are several problems with this assumption. First, the size of a nation's population may indicate the potential size of its military, if it implemented a draft for mandatory service, but this was not the case for any of the Arab states. Israel was the only state with a national policy of mandatory military service for all draft age men and women. Israel possessed a well-trained citizen army, ready to fight when the need arose no matter how ill-equipped they may have been.

The Arab states, on the other hand, had only recently become independent nations free of colonial control, giving them little time to have raised, trained, and equipped a nationalist army of any great strength. Colonial powers are rarely interested in building a strong nationalist military with nationalist commanders among the people they work so hard to control. Most of the Arab states, apart from Jordan, had no prior combat experience.[37] None of them were prepared for war.[38] The ragtag armies of Syria and Lebanon participated only marginally in Israel's northern border regions; in fact, the Lebanese forces spent most of the war in a defensive posture dug in behind its own border.[39] Saudi Arabia had no regular army at all; their irregular volunteer troops had only a marginal supply of ammunition and ended up as an auxiliary force with the Egyptians. Even though the Egyptians had the largest of the Arab armies at the beginning of the Arab War, only a fragment of its units had adequate training to be sent to the front. Egypt, Iraq, and Syria were all confronted with massive, public demonstrations sparked by the Partition Plan, demanding that the Palestinians be rescued from the UN's support of a Zionist state. A major reason these nations were sending any troops into combat was the governments' fears of revolution fomented by the numerous popular uprisings demanding military action. Regarding Egypt, the military advisor in the British

35. Morris, *Righteous Victims*, 192.

36. Lieutenant General John Glubb, commander of the Jordanian Arab Legion, rehearses, only to debunk, "the common impression that the heroic little Israeli army was fighting against tremendous odds"—one nation against five; see his memoir, *Soldier with the Arabs*, 195.

37. Pappé, *Making*, 108. This section of the chapter largely depends on Pappé's discussion "The Balance of Power" on pp. 108–13 of *Making*.

38. Morris, *Righteous Victims*, 219.

39. Morris, *1948*, 189, 194.

embassy in Cairo warned that, despite these vehement public outcries, "the Egyptian army hardly warrants consideration as a serious invading force."[40]

The Arab Legion of Jordan[41] was the only Arab army of any significance capable of standing against the Jewish forces. It was the only Arab military that enjoyed a consistent training program "as well as an adequate maintenance level."[42] However, their involvement in the Palestine war was severely compromised by the political intrigue surrounding the Jordanian king's passion to expand his territorial holdings throughout Palestine and beyond (discussed in the next section).

When the Arab armies attacked on May 15, 1948, approximately ten thousand Egyptian troops were joined by three thousand Syrians, three thousand Iraqis, fewer than one thousand Lebanese, two thousand Arab volunteers, and forty-five hundred members of the Jordanian Arab Legion. These forces were added to the twelve thousand Palestinian fighters already engaged with the Jewish military. On May 1, 1948, the Israeli prime minister was told by the chief of the army personnel department that they had a fighting force of 22,425; as of June 4, 1948, that number had risen to 35,368; by mid-July the IDF mobilized 65,000 men, and by the end of December their forces had reached a peak of 96,441 troops, all well armed.[43] We see that at the beginning of the Arab war an uncoordinated, disparate force of 35,500 Arab troops with no real unitary command were meeting a comparably sized, well-trained, well-equipped Zionist military already operating in well-studied terrain. Not only were the Israeli forces not outnumbered, but by the second stage of the war the Arab armies were increasingly outmatched by superior Israeli forces (by a ratio of well over two to one) as well as superior firepower. In the words of new historian Avi Shlaim, "The final outcome of the war was therefore not a miracle but a faithful reflection of the underlying military balance in the Palestine theater. In this war, as in most wars, the stronger side prevailed."[44]

40. Pappé, *Making*, 109.

41. At the time, the state now called Jordan was called Transjordan. I am referring to Jordan for simplicity's sake.

42. Pappé, *Making*, 110.

43. Shlaim, "Israel and the Arab," 81.

44. Shlaim, "Israel and the Arab," 81.

The Unexpected Effects of Arab-Zionist Politics

The Jordanian Arab Legion remained the wild card in the Arab deck. Unbeknownst to the other Arab leaders, King Abdullah of Jordan had conducted a series of secret meetings with Zionist leaders from the Jewish Agency, including future Israeli Prime Minister Golda Meir.[45] The subject of these meetings was a Jordanian–Zionist partition plan which would divide Palestine between the Jews and the kingdom of Jordan. It was, in effect, a non-aggression pact, and it would finally determine the outcome of the war.[46] King Abdullah was promised the territory that had been committed to an Arab state in the UN Partition plan, largely the area now known as the West Bank. In return, Abdullah promised to limit his troop deployments to that territory. He also promised not to attack Jewish forces in the territory designated for the Jewish state,[47] while Jewish leaders promised not to attack Jordanian forces in the West Bank.[48] This territorial agreement would partially fulfill King Abdullah's dreams of ruling over a Greater Syria comprising Jordan, Palestine, Syria, and Lebanon. However, the Zionist leadership was determined to make Jerusalem the capital of their newfound state. Despite the fact that Jerusalem is located in the West Bank, Jewish troops attacked the Old City. Jordanian forces counter-attacked. Fierce battles ensued between Jordanian and Zionist forces in east Jerusalem and the surrounding region.[49] In part, this was due to Jerusalem's designation as an international zone with no clear attribution of Arab or Jewish sovereignty. Eventually, Jordan limited the Jewish advance to the western half of the city, retaining east Jerusalem (with the Old City) as a part of the West Bank. Israeli forces, on the other hand, violated their non-aggression treaty with Jordan by capturing, keeping, or destroying many Arab villages that lay within the UN borders of the future Arab state.[50] Despite this Zionist

45. For the definitive history of these negotiations and their impact on the Palestine war, see Shlaim, *Collusion Across the Jordan*; also Shlaim, *Politics*, 39–53; Morris, *Righteous Victims*, 221–23.

46. Pappé, *Making*, 115.

47. Pappé, *Making*, 119; Shlaim, "Israel and the Arab," 86.

48. Pappé, *Making*, 119.

49. Shlaim, *Iron Wall*, 36–37.

50. Flapan, *Birth*, 198–99, offers an interesting analysis of Israeli fatalities during the war. He notes that more Israeli soldiers died while attacking (50 percent) than while defending against attacks (21 percent). Sixty percent of all Jewish casualties occurred while attacking Arab villages and related areas in regions designated for an Arab state.

betrayal, King Abdullah kept his word, and the Jordanian Arab Legion, the most capable army in the Arab alliance, never attacked a Jewish settlement in Jewish-designated territory.

Arab Lack of Cooperation

Professors Eugene Rogan and Avi Shlaim, both of Oxford University, have edited a fascinating book, titled *The War for Palestine*, that examines the internal affairs, military strength, and international relationships of the Arab states that attacked Israel in 1948. The book's contributors describe in great detail the fact that these five Arab armies were a "coalition" that never coalesced. From beginning to end, they remained independent forces separated by deep, mutual suspicions, leading to a refusal to cooperate and an insistence on prioritizing their own national ambitions above and beyond the formation of any unified attack against Israel. So extreme were these shared hostilities that Avi Shlaim can say, "Arab disunity provided [Israel] the strategic luxury of fighting a war on only one front at a time."[51]

The principal fly in the Arab ointment, of course, was King Abdullah of Jordan. His secret alliance with Israel allowed him to pursue his personal vision of a Greater Syria and focus his military efforts on protecting his territorial gains in the West Bank, while refusing to cooperate with Arab strategies (as feeble as they might be) for attacking the nascent Jewish state. Of course, these actions, combined with rumors hinting at his secret meetings with representatives of the Jewish Agency, caused his would-be allies to thoroughly distrust the intentions of the Jordanian army. It is no exaggeration to say that the other Arab leaders expended more energy in strategizing ways to block King Abdullah and contain his ambitions in Palestine than they did in trying to stop the creation of a Jewish state. For instance, to summarize the battlefield situation in 1948, Charles Tripp, professor of politics at the University of London, writes with respect to Iraq, "Despite being the largest single Arab force in Palestine by the end of the war, Iraq did little beyond occupying defensive positions in the hills of the West Bank."[52]

Egypt entered the war with no advance planning and a misjudgment of their enemy. "The Egyptian regime had no appreciation of the complexity and danger of its military adventure, and saw it . . . as a police action to

51. Shlaim, "Israel and the Arab," 98.

52. Tripp, "Iraq," 125.

punish 'the Zionist gangs.'" Some assumed that these "gangs" would drop their weapons and run away as soon as the Egyptian army entered the field. "This was a classic case of how cultural misperceptions blinded officials and distorted their analysis," writes Professor Fawaz Gerges of Sarah Lawrence College.[53] Similar summaries can be offered to describe the positions of Lebanon and Syria, who also were more fearful of King Abdullah's regional ambitions than they were of a fledgling Jewish state. Matthew Hughes of Brunel University concludes that for this reason "Lebanon did very little to confront Israel; nor did it do much to help Arab irregular forces fighting across the border in Galilee."[54] For Syria, "the real danger was the prospect that it [i.e., Abdullah's agreement with the Jewish Agency] would allow the Hashemites [i.e., the Jordanian ruling family] to become the dominant power in the region. . . . From the beginning, the fight was over the balance of power [among the Arabs] . . . this was not a war waged to destroy the Jewish state."[55]

The Negative Effects of Overblown Rhetoric

At the time, Arab leaders were given to extremely bellicose, over-heated rhetoric about the impending Arab annihilation of the Zionist army. But their actions never came close to measuring up to their public bluster, which was primarily intended for domestic consumption. The real purpose of this inflammatory political speech was not accurately to report battlefield conditions but to strengthen their own political positions, stirring up the masses to demonstrate in the streets showing their support back home. However, the Jewish immigrants to Israel, who had only recently escaped the Nazi Holocaust in Europe, had every reason to panic when hearing these threats of annihilation[56] from Arab leaders during the Palestine war. They had recently seen how a dictator's boasts about Jewish annihilation may come to pass in mass slaughter. How were they to know that these

53. Gerges, "Egypt," 158.

54. Hughes, "Collusion," 219.

55. Landis, "Syria," 176.

56. At this point it is important to remember the evidence presented in chapter 3. These were calls for the elimination of political Zionism from Palestine, not for the elimination of all Jews.

Arab leaders were merely strutting and crowing like barnyard roosters? At the time, their fears were well founded.[57]

However, there is no excuse for perpetuating these sorts of exaggerations today. Such language is far removed from the historical evidence as we now know it and is equally removed from current realities. David Brog remains the poster child for recklessly repeating 1948 fears of "annihilation" in today's context where the new history has demonstrated that those fears were always unwarranted. No Arab state was capable of, nor did any Arab state have the intention of, annihilating all the Jews of Palestine. Yet, Brog, and others like him, persist in deploying this highly inflammatory and wholly unsuitable language when he repeats descriptions of the 1948 war as Israel's desperate struggle for survival,[58] its war of extermination,[59] threatening likely physical annihilation,[60] and the Jewish impending massacre.[61] What began as an understandable but baseless fear in a cross-cultural setting where neither side understood the other has now become a rhetorical tool in Zionist efforts to stoke an undying public image of Jews as perpetual victims, perennially threatened by the next pogrom of complete destruction wherever they go, no matter the era or context. Such hysterical paranoia today only serves the interests of those who want to stoke irrational fear, perpetual antagonism, and racist suspicions.

One of the goals of good history writing should be the deconstruction of such false consciousness and the unfettered paranoia that results when false history sustains ahistorical bogeymen. Christian Zionists loyal to Israel would do well to embrace the new history, rooted as it is in a deeper, broader measure of historical evidence. Doing so does not make one "anti-Israel," as the revivers of the old history contend. But it does make one a more accurately informed participant in an ongoing historical conversation with important implications for the way Jews, Arabs, and their confederates view each other today.

57. These fears of annihilation were also based on the cross-cultural misunderstandings that arose because European Ashkenazi Jews did not understand the history of ecumenical coexistence between Middle Eastern Mizrahi Jews and Palestinian Arabs.

58. Brog, *Reclaiming*, 125.

59. Brog, *Reclaiming*, 126.

60. Brog, *Reclaiming*, 131.

61. Brog, *Reclaiming*, 133.

Conclusion

Many evangelical Christians cling to the story of Israel's miraculous victory in the 1948–1949 war because it conveniently serves the purposes of Christian apologetics.[62] The tale of an Israeli David defeating the Arab Goliath plays well to an evangelical audience eager to hear evidence justifying the valorization of Israel and a belief in the reliability of holy Scripture. Yet, the work of the new historians and their followers have proven that this traditional story about an Israeli victory against overwhelming odds is another piece, a central piece, of Zionist mythology. The truth is that Israel won the war because they had the stronger military force. Acknowledging this historical fact does not threaten the authority of Scripture or the truth of the gospel. In fact, the integrity of the church's witness is diminished when evangelicals conspire with Zionist storylines now known to be unhistorical misrepresentations of what actually happened.

62. Christian apologetics generally involves the empirical defense of the Christian faith.

MYTH #5

Israel's Military Is the Most Moral Army in the World

It is not unusual to hear Israel's army, the Israel Defense Forces (IDF), described as the most moral army in the world by authors and commentators discussing Israeli military operations in the West Bank, Gaza, Lebanon, or Syria. Only last week I was watching a televised debate on the question of whether Israel was guilty of genocide in Gaza. The advocate arguing in favor of this charge presented a litany of heinous evidence—the bombing of Gazan tent cities, the dozens of children now dying of starvation, and the many people shot as they wait in line for food at Gaza Humanitarian Foundation distribution sites—all weighing in favor of the prosecution.

Into the midst of the prosecution's case, the woman tasked with defending Israel's innocence suddenly blurted out, "Israel has the most moral army in the world!" Rather than citing contrary evidence or rehearsing the statements of reputable human rights organizations contesting the charge of genocide, she chose to cite what she obviously believed to be a definitive slogan: The Israeli military is the most moral army in the world. The claim seemed so self-evident to her (and to many like her) that it is simply beyond the realm of possibility to consider that Israel's most moral army could ever be guilty of genocide.

Setting aside for a moment the problems inherent in offering a statement of national identity as evidence in a debate, we cannot help but wonder what it means for any army to claim that it is the most moral in the world. No one knows who first attributed this vaulted status to the IDF, but I confess that when I first heard this claim years ago it struck me as the height of duplicitous arrogance. Since when do armies compete for the title of "most moral"? I would argue that this claim is an oxymoron; it is an inherent contradiction for any military to wrap itself in a cloak of moral superiority. All warfare is ultimately the failure of collective morality—regardless of what one thinks about the righteousness of self-defense. Beyond the inherent contradiction at its root, even if someone sought to make this case, how does anyone even begin to gauge the *most* moral army of them all? What are the possible standards of measurement? And who gets to hold the measuring tape? After all, is it not dubious to refer to anything as the most (most good looking, most intelligent) when the claim is self-referential?

After some reflection, one could be forgiven for suggesting that international humanitarian law, also known as the laws of armed combat, should serve as the universal standard for measuring military morality in combat for all nations. It seems the obvious solution. But as with so many of the other subjects discussed in this book, the Jewish state of Israel has never been comfortable with this universal standard of measurement and instead has preferred to devise a unique standard of its own.

The IDF and the Purity of Arms

Extraordinary claims require extraordinary standards and compelling evidence to prove their merit. The standards the IDF uses to uphold the claim of "most moral army" are ill defined and thus allow for a wide range of moral plasticity, as we will see below. The IDF claim to superlative morality—a status regularly defined as "purity of arms"—emerged in the early days of the Arab Revolt (1936–1939), long before claims of moral supremacy were attributed to the IDF. In 1937, Britain began to arm and to train Jewish troops to fight alongside the British Mandatory forces so they could assist in suppressing an anti-Zionist, Palestinian/Arab rebellion. This training prompted fierce debate among Zionist factions concerning the posture Jewish forces should adopt in fighting alongside the British. Jewish soldiers were being trained in the aggressive, all-or-nothing counter-insurgency tactics employed by British captain Orde Wingate and his Special Night Squads.[1] Wingate was a zealous Christian Zionist who openly despised Arabs. His Special Night Squads were trained in counter-insurgency tactics that many disapproved of. A fellow British officer described Wingate as "a

1. Chazan, "Dispute in Mapai," 105; Hughes, "Terror in Galilee."

dangerous madman" whose madness infected his fighting methods.[2] Wingate regularly attacked the Arab enemy with overwhelming surprise attacks; felt no compunction about killing civilians, including women and children; practiced wanton, collective punishment; was adept at the use of torture; demolished civilian homes and businesses at will; and regularly executed prisoners. He was a terrorist in an army uniform.

Wingate's brutal tactics certainly raised questions among his fellow officers, but the Jewish troops under his command developed a reverent devotion for their British captain because they knew full well that he was laying the foundations for the future Israeli army. To list only one of several possible examples, Moshe Dayan (1915–1981), a veteran leader in the 1948 war who eventually became Israel's minister of defense, trained under Wingate and was impressed by his "utter ruthlessness" and his "willingness to shoot Arabs on the spot to make an example for others."[3] Dayan maintained a lifelong affection for Wingate "that knew no bounds," an affection that continued to shape Dayan's own views on fighting Arabs throughout his military and political career. Wingate's methods were also endorsed by Ze'ev Jabotinsky, leader of the Revisionist party, ancestors of today's conservative Likud party in Israel. With this heritage, it's perhaps unsurprising that the Likud have always rejected any possibility for a future Palestinian state.

By the fall of 1938 the Mandatory government had developed enough trepidation over Wingate's fighting methods that he was reassigned from Palestine to the Sudan where he created guerilla forces to combat Italy's colonization of Ethiopia. In Wingate's absence, the Special Night Squad units he founded in Israel were disbanded. However, as we will see, Wingate's influence and the heritage of the Special Night Squads continued to cast a long, dark shadow over the emerging Israeli military.

Military Public Relations

Unlike Jabotinsky and the right-wing Revisionist party, the left-wing Labor Zionists, keeping in step with the ethos of British Mandatory officials, demanded a more measured, restrained approach to armed conflict even though few of them had ever publicly objected to Captain Wingate's ruthless methods. David Ben-Gurion, leader of the liberal Labor Zionist

2. Hughes, "Terror in Galilee," 604.

3. Hughes, "Terror in Galilee," 604.

movement, was the principal advocate for Labor's alternative perspective, a philosophy of military restraint referred to as purity of arms.[4] However, Labor Zionism's motives for objecting to the Revisionist/Wingate perspective on Jewish military methods were not rooted in any moral qualms about the use of excessive violence. Their objections reflected more pragmatic, political considerations. Ben-Gurion's focus was on the careful shepherding of an embryonic Jewish state that remained under the tutelage of its British Mandatory overseers. He feared that a Jewish military in Mandate Palestine must not appear to be overly aggressive. Any actions that might fan the flames of an unruly Arab revolt would only provide Zionism's enemies with additional opportunities to blame this regional conflict on the pressures created by increasing Jewish immigration. Even though the accelerated rate of Jewish immigration was in fact at the heart of Arab/Palestinian protests, Ben-Gurion and his fellow Labor party leaders wanted to blur any connection between the Palestinian revolt and aggressive Zionist colonial settlement. Using the language of the doctrine of purity of arms—with vague and subjective notions of self-control, restraint, and fighting only in self-defense as supposed earmarks of Jewish military engagement with the Palestinians—Labor leaders then painted Palestinians as "rebellious Arabs," irrational aggressors attacking an orderly, peace-loving community of Zionist immigrants.

Labor leaders insisted that the fledgling Jewish community must always appear to observers as the small, innocent victim forced to defend itself against unprovoked Arab aggression—a plotline as useful today as it was in 1937 when the phrase "purity of arms" was first used. As the historian Meir Chazan has explained,

> It was not the moral-cultural aspect that determined [the Labor party's] preference for a policy of restraint. Most important to [Labor] were the political considerations of a national movement for which quiet and stability were essential conditions for its continued activity.[5]

Initially, the vague term "purity of arms" was more of a public relations slogan than a concrete code of conduct. Leaders like Ben-Gurion worried about maintaining Zionism's public image as a movement that

4. "Purity of arms emerged on the background of a strident left/right debate among various wings of the Zionist movement"; Zion, "Purity of Arms," 16.

5. For the several related political concerns that fueled Ben-Gurion's pragmatism, see Chazan, "Dispute in Mapai," 92–93.

avoided conflict whenever possible and only took up arms in self-defense, thus keeping their weapons pure. Orde Wingate, however, had instilled utterly impure fighting methods into the newly formed Jewish militias. The official military rhetoric did not cohere with the military's actual behavior. Zionist troops had been inducted into ruthless fighting methods which are often deployed by imperial powers. Well-practiced ways of eradicating native resistance, finely honed throughout the long history of the British Empire, had been handed down to a fledgling Jewish military as they encountered indigenous Palestinian resistance to Zionist settlement.[6] Labor Zionist claims of deploying a military restrained by purity of arms were nothing more than rhetorical subterfuge. Tragically, the vast chasm separating stated policy from military reality was as deep as it was dark.

The Spirit of the IDF

The first written IDF code of conduct was produced in 1994, nearly sixty years after the phrase "purity of arms" hinted at a moral code that had no grounding in fact or practice. That code was revised in 2001 in the early days of the Second Intifada as a response to the growing number of young Israelis who refused to join the IDF's mission of enforcing Israel's military occupation in Gaza and the West Bank.[7] This revision, which was amended again in 2005, lays out the principles for maintaining purity of arms and was titled "The Spirit of the IDF."[8] The opening section states that the IDF's view of morality in combat is drawn from four sources: the military heritage of the IDF; the legal traditions and principles of the state of Israel; the historical traditions of the Jewish people; and universal moral values based on the dignity of human life. Space does not allow for an in-depth analysis of all the principles laid out in this document; I will simply draw a few observations about the four sources listed above and then refer to one additional point made by Muhammad Ali Khalidi, Presidential Professor of Philosophy at City University of New York Graduate Center, in his

6. See Elkins, *Legacy of Violence*, 221–28.

7. M. Khalidi, "Most Moral Army," 7; also see Zion, "Purity of Arms," 3. Khalidi's article in the *Journal of Palestine Studies* is required reading for anyone who hopes to understand not only the history of Israel's claim to be defended by the most moral army in the world but also the ways in which Israel justifies ignoring international humanitarian law on the battlefield.

8. See Jewish Virtual Library, "Israel Defense Forces."

insightful article "'The Most Moral Army in the World': The New 'Ethical Code' of the Israeli Military and the War on Gaza."[9]

First of all, it is significant that seventy-six years after the signing of the Fourth Geneva Convention (in 1949) and nearly fifty years after Protocols I and II were added to the Convention (in 1977) the "Spirit of the IDF" documents make no reference to international law but instead root their authority in unspecified "universal moral values" and the "dignity of human life," principles that are quite vague and subject to a variety of interpretations.[10] Although the infant state of Israel signed the Fourth Geneva Convention in 1949—as a newly admitted member to the United Nations, it could hardly do otherwise—it still refuses (together with the United States) to sign the 1977 Protocols I and II, which deal largely with the treatment of civilians and the management of occupied enemy territory. Given the outcome of the Six-Day War in 1967, it is no accident that Israel will not sign the principal documents of international humanitarian law that condemn the belligerent occupation of territory captured in war. By 1977 the IDF had occupied captured Palestinian territory in Gaza, the West Bank, and the Golan Heights for a decade, showing no sign of ever abiding by the terms of the Hague Convention, the Geneva Convention Protocols, and the numerous United Nations resolutions which forbid such military occupation.

My second observation notes the self-referential—one could say self-justifying—nature of the first three purity of arms principles. The IDF says it is committed to drawing from the heritage of the IDF, of the state of Israel, and of Jewish tradition. However, pressing questions which are never addressed in "The Spirit of the IDF" surround all three of these as sources for military morality.

To begin with, Orde Wingate and his legacy of bloodthirsty ruthlessness continue to play a prominent role in the modern ethos of the IDF. Numerous Israeli organizations and military institutions regularly celebrate Wingate's memory and boast about their efforts to keep his legacy alive. Michael Oren, an Israeli historian and Knesset member, has proclaimed that "Wingate was the father of the IDF. The IDF today remains Wingatean in terms of its tactics."[11] In my view, this is an astonishing admission. Remember that Wingatean tactics involved much more than surprise attacks

9. See note 7.

10. See M. Khalidi, "Most Moral Army," 7.

11. Kuttler, "75 Years After His Death."

after dark; they include collective punishment and an indiscriminate use of force that ignores the distinction—a fundamental distinction demanded by international law—between military and civilian targets, active-duty soldiers and innocent noncombatants. Wingatean tactics not only allow for but encourage attacks against anything that might potentially be used by the enemy, including hospitals, schools, homes, universities, water treatment plants, bakeries, food distribution centers, you name it. To valorize Orde Wingate is publicly to repudiate the importance of moral scruples on the battlefield. A society that venerates an unhinged war criminal like Wingate is incapable of grasping the value of international humanitarian law much less following it.

Thirdly, we cannot forget that the IDF is a citizen's army. Every Jewish member of Israeli society, both male and female, is compelled to join the military upon high school graduation. The educational system prepares students for their eventual IDF service from a young age, teaching Jewish school children about the honorable service that awaits them at age eighteen. The mentality of Israeli society is broadly influenced by the mentality of the IDF; the ethos of the IDF is pervasive throughout Israeli society.[12] It is the worldview consistently impressed upon every Israeli's youthful character during their most formative years. Israeli sociologist Baruch Kimmerling referred to this worldview as "cognitive militarism: a world view in which civil society adopts, wholesale, the way of thinking of the military. Civilians are military in waiting."[13]

The number of Israelis who have gone to prison as conscientious objectors after refusing to perform their tour of duty in the Israeli military is extremely small.[14] A Pew Research poll reveals that nearly three-quarters (73 percent) of the Israeli public believes that Israel's military response in Gaza—a response that many have described as ethnic cleansing and genocide—has been "about right" (39 percent) or "not gone far enough" (34 percent).[15] A poll commissioned by Pennsylvania State University found

12. See the numerous essays by Israeli journalist Gideon Levy describing Israeli society's lack of conscience post–October 7. The dehumanization of Palestinians as "the enemy" is pervasive; see *Killing*, 137–39; 155–57; 178–80; 187–89; 194–96; 199–200; 203–5; 216–18; 228–30; 261–63; 287–89.

13. Peled-Elhanan, *Holocaust Education*, 4.

14. Precise figures are impossible to find given the nature of the process. It is not something the Israeli government or the IDF want to publicize.

15. The poll was conducted in the spring of 2014; see Silver and Smerkovick, "Israeli Views."

that 70 percent of the secular, Jewish Israeli public supports the mass expulsion, i.e., the ethnic cleansing, of all Palestinians from Gaza; that figure rose to 90 percent among religious and Orthodox Jews (who do not serve in the IDF).[16] Ninety-one percent of Jewish men under forty, that is men serving either in the army reserves or on active duty with the IDF, are in favor of ethnic cleansing. When asked if the IDF should follow the model provided by the ancient Israelites in killing all a city's residents after capturing that city, 47 percent of Israeli Jews answered yes. Contemporary history is now illustrating the fact that when it comes to conduct on the battlefield the moral heritage of the entire Israeli state as well as that of the IDF are not only coterminous but equally bankrupt.[17]

Another principal source of military ethics listed in "The Spirit of the IDF" is the legacy of Jewish tradition. However, aside from a handful of brief periods of Jewish rebellion in ancient history, all of them squashed by the Roman Empire, Israel has no significant military history, no long-standing tradition of national Jewish armies in need of moral boundaries or codes of conduct. "For most of Jewish history . . . the laws of combat were merely theoretical. There were no Jewish armies and no Jewish wars. Therefore, practical ethics of war are not often discussed in Talmudic and medieval Jewish literature."[18] Rabbinic tradition about warfare is sparse yet diverse with an important tension at its center. Protecting civilian life is a crucial concern, yet rules of discrimination are subordinate to the greater priority of self-defense. "When you go to war, your priority must be killing your enemies," explains rabbi Shlomo Brody, author of the book *Ethics of Our Fighters: A Jewish View of War and Morality*. In fact, leaving mortal enemies alive to fight another day is a "moral failing," even if killing them involves the collateral deaths of civilians.[19] This rabbinical emphasis on the unmitigated priority of Jewish self-defense suggests that the IDF's designation as the most moral army in the world is a self-evident conclusion when viewed from within a rabbinical ethical framework. In other words, IDF morality is not a function of military tactics or strategy or the laws of discrimination and proportionality. Rather, the standard of superior IDF morality is embedded within the IDF mission: to defend the Jewish state. This is the most moral objective that any Jewish soldier can take on—the

16. Rapaport, "Nearly Half."

17. See note 12.

18. Hoffman, "Jewish Commandments."

19. Brody, "What Does the Torah Have to Say," paras. 20 and 23.

defense of fellow Jews. The lesson is tautological. The IDF is the most moral army in the world simply because it is the Israel Defense Forces, and nothing is more important for a Jewish fighter than defending the Jewish state.

Since October 7, vengeful statements made by Israeli public figures have drawn largely from two Old Testament traditions: Joshua's eradication of the Canaanites during the Israelite conquest of the "promised land" (see Deut 7); and God's command to slaughter the Amalekites, including women, children, and livestock (1 Sam 15:3).[20] It is noteworthy that both incidents in the Hebrew Scriptures sanction genocide against Israel's enemies, a connection that has not gone unnoticed by the Israeli public and its leaders. Benjamin Netanyahu, Israel's prime minister, along with several other Israeli public figures, have drawn on these traditions and publicly called for all Israelis to "remember what Amalek has done to you" in reference to the Hamas attack. These are obvious calls for the people of Gaza to be treated as ancient Israel treated the Amalekites.[21] Knesset member Ariel Kallner called for a "Nakba that will overshadow the Nakba of '48" to be unleashed upon Gaza.[22] Another member of the Knesset, Tally Gotliv, called for "not flattening a neighborhood" but "crushing and flattening Gaza without mercy."[23] During a press conference on October 13, 2023, Israel's president, Isaac Herzog, insisted that it was not only Hamas but "an entire nation out there that is responsible," justifying a genocidal assault against all the people of Gaza.[24]

The devout Christian Zionist Orde Wingate had drunk deeply from these same Old Testament, Hebrew traditions. His personal hero was the biblical figure Gideon who led his own campaigns to eliminate Canaanite enemies. The genocidal, biblical traditions that animated Wingate remain embedded in the IDF and the whole of Israeli society today. In the words of Israeli journalist Nadav Rapaport, the Hamas attack on October 7 "unleashed demons that have been nurtured over decades in the media and in the [Israeli] legal and educational systems."[25]

20. Hasson and Maanit, "Lost Battle."

21. Wilkins, "Netanyahu Accused," para. 2.

22. *Middle East Monitor*, "Israel MK Calls," para. 2.

23. Wilkins, "'We Are Too Humane,'" para. 12.

24. Blumenthal, "Israeli President," para. 2.

25. Rapaport, "Nearly Half."

The IDF and Civilian Casualties

I will underscore one final point that has been noted by Khalidi's analysis of "The Spirit of the IDF"; that is, its explicit demotion of the military's duty to protect civilian noncombatants. From the four fundamental values discussed above, "The Spirit of the IDF" derives "ten additional values." The fourth and fifth of these additional values are the value of human life and purity of arms.[26]

Under the heading of "Human Life" the document reads, "An IDF soldier will recognize the critical importance of human life and behave in a safe and measured manner at all times. During combat the soldier will put themselves and their fellow soldiers at risk only to the extent required to fulfill their mission." Under the following heading, "Purity of Arms," we read, "An IDF soldier . . . will maintain their humanity during combat and routine times. The soldier will not use their weapon or power to harm uninvolved civilians and prisoners."[27]

Both the language and ordering of these statements are important. First, notice that the value of human life focuses on the ultimate value of IDF life; it is the soldiers "themselves and their fellow soldiers" whose lives have supreme value. The soldier's life is given the highest priority in combat. IDF fighters are to think about protecting themselves and their comrades first and foremost, an ordering of values very much in line with the rabbinic perspective on the priority of Jewish self-defense noted earlier. As Brody observes, "Protecting soldiers is the highest priority . . . we [the IDF] cannot be held responsible for collateral damage."[28] "Force protection . . . is a deep moral obligation. There is no compelling reason why the state should jeopardize their [soldiers'] lives to save the terrorist's neighbor. . . . When push comes to shove, brother trumps other."[29] The consideration of civilian lives and their protection—falling under the "Purity of Arms"—comes *after*

26. The ten additional values listed in the IDF mission statement are perseverance in the mission and pursuit of victory, responsibility, reliability and trustworthiness, personal example, human life, purity of arms, professionalism, discipline, camaraderie, a sense of mission.

27. Israel Defense Forces, "Our Mission."

28. Brody, *Ethics of Our Fighters*, 252.

29. Brody, *Ethics of Our Fighters*, 293. Brody (291–302) offers an extensive defense of this position wherein Jewish self-preservation must always trump the protection of noncombatants. This section is headed "Brother over Other: Force Protection as a Superior Moral Value."

the safeguarding of military life, and even this consideration has a condition placed on it. A concern for human life is extended only to "uninvolved civilians," however that subjective determination may be made by the attacking soldiers. The problem is that both considerations—prioritizing military over civilian life and protecting only "uninvolved" civilians—are blatant violations of international humanitarian law.[30]

The Fourth Geneva Convention applies *the principle of distinction*, separating civilians from combatants, absolutely without exception. Calculating civilian "involvement" is not a consideration. The basic rule of Protocol I, article 48 states,

> In order to ensure respect for and protection of the civilian population and civilian objects, the Parties to the conflict shall at all times distinguish between the civilian population and combatants and between civilian objects and military objectives and accordingly shall direct their operations only against military objectives.

This absolute principle of distinction is repeated and elaborated at several points in Protocol I (see articles 50, 51, 52, 54, 57). Article 57 is particularly emphatic. Point 2.a.i insists that the attacker must do "everything feasible" to ensure that civilians are not harmed. Both subsections 2.a.ii and 2.a.iii require that all means necessary be taken to avoid even "the incidental loss of civilian life" which would be excessive in relation to the military advantage expected. These appeals to *the principle of proportionality* both place the greater weight of consideration on the side of civilian protection. According to the Geneva Convention, even "incidental" damage to or loss of civilian life is considered a disproportionate loss making the attack illegal and unethical. Protecting civilians from injury is the prime directive.

Having now briefly examined several ways in which the IDF's own code of conduct, the purity of arms and "The Spirit of the IDF," flagrantly depart from the most basic standards of international humanitarian law, we will now look at one specific arena where the IDF's disregard for international law and basic human rights are displayed publicly.

30. M. Khalidi, "Most Moral Army," 11–14.

The IDF and the Occupied Palestinian Territories[31]

> Inhabitants of Aida, we are the occupation's army. If you continue to throw stones, we will continue to shoot gas until you die, the children, the adults, the elderly, the dying. Everything. We do not want to leave any of you alive. . . . We will shoot gas until you die: on your homes, on your families, brothers, sons, everything.

This message was broadcast from an armored personnel carrier throughout the Aida refugee camp on the outskirts of Bethlehem in October 2015.[32] The soldiers warned that they were holding a young man captive at their military base just opposite the camp on the other side of the Separation Wall, a barrier that delineates the camp's northern boundary. The soldiers were threatening their Palestinian hostage with public execution if the camp's residents did not comply with their threatening orders.

Aida residents are consistently victimized by this "occupation army." Soldiers periodically roam the streets, firing tear gas into the homes, aiming for open doors and windows. At least one asthmatic woman, a young mother who had recently given birth, was murdered by the soldiers who shot a tear gas canister into her living room. The gas sparked a fatal asthma attack as she was caring for her baby. No IDF personnel ever stopped by to apologize to the grieving family, to take responsibility, or to offer compensation. They never do.

My friend Mohammed was shot in the face as he stood on his apartment's balcony taking photographs of IDF soldiers firing tear gas in the streets.[33] After several reconstructive surgeries, he decided to sue the IDF. His case has never made any headway in the IDF's military court system, but Israeli soldiers have visited his home where they beat him mercilessly, giving extra attention to the seeping bandages covering his sutures and broken bones.

My friend Said was giving me a tour of his home. As Said took me to the second-story balcony on the back of the house, I couldn't help but notice numerous bullet holes circling the window looking out onto the balcony.

31. The stories in this section are all drawn from my contacts, friends, and personal experiences in the occupied territory called the West Bank.

32. See al-Ozza and Hallowell, *Forced Population Transfer*, 28; Crump, *Like Birds in a Cage*, 74.

33. For more on Mohammed's story, see Crump, *Like Birds in a Cage*, 64–71. The book contains many more stories about additional IDF crimes against Palestinians.

Said explained that the holes were made by the Israeli soldiers who used his home for target practice, shooting from the nearby IDF base. Fortunately, few bullets had ever made it into the family room. Apparently, not many of the soldiers were crack shots. However, Said was once shot while standing in the doorway. The bullet entered his left shoulder just missing his heart. I imagine the shooter was aiming for his heart but thankfully missed his target just as many others had missed the family room window.

These short stories describe Palestinian life under Israeli military occupation. I could multiply them many times over. My brief accounts are only a tiny fraction of the innumerable, tragic horror stories that Palestinians can tell about Israeli oppression and the cavalier manner in which the young men and women of the IDF dole out mayhem, injury, trauma, and death to innocent people who are only trying to live their lives.

The IDF has an official name for this strategy ensuring that even the most mundane affairs of daily life might careen unexpectedly onto the edge of potential catastrophe: They call it the searing of consciousness.[34] It is a weaponization of the psychological condition psychologists call learned helplessness.[35] When a caged dog is given random electric shocks, unpredictable punishments that have no rhyme or reason, it will eventually adopt an attitude of futility. The dog will curl up in the corner shivering. It will lay there passively, not moving anywhere even when shocked, for there is no perceivable pattern to what will bring the pain.

The IDF leadership has consciously developed their own program of learned helplessness toward the people living in the occupied territories. The occupation is a cage. The Palestinians are treated as lab animals on whom Israel experiments with continual, random shocks of violence. Breaking the Silence describes this searing of consciousness methodology as one the "cornerstones of IDF strategy."[36] One of the cornerstones! It justifies "the assumption that distinguishing between enemy civilians and enemy combatants is not necessary . . . systematic harm to Palestinians as a whole makes the population more obedient and easier to control."[37]

The Hamas attack on October 7, 2023, has reminded Israel that human beings are not dogs. Some, at least, will inevitably shake off their learned helplessness and rise up. The same lesson may be drawn from the citizen

34. Breaking the Silence, *Our Harsh Logic*, 9–11.

35. See my discussion in Crump, *Like Birds in a Cage*, 163–64.

36. Breaking the Silence, *Our Harsh Logic*, 9.

37. Breaking the Silence, *Our Harsh Logic*, 11.

rebellions, called the First (1987–1993) and Second (2000–2005) Intifadas, that broke out in the West Bank. All three incidents remind us that no matter how severely mistreated, subjugated people will not cower in the corner forever. On October 7, Israel suffered the reactionary wrath of a population they had caged, shocked, beaten, and mistreated for many decades. In 2005 Israel constructed a seven-meter wall with sensors and remote-controlled machine guns surrounding Gaza. This confinement included devastating, periodic military attacks referred to as "mowing the lawn." What more needs to be said about IDF inhumanity when Palestinians are dehumanized, considered as being of as little value as blades of grass in need of "mowing"—a most heartless euphemism for slaughter if there ever was one. The Palestinian consciousness may have been traumatized and seared, but it remained a human consciousness, damaged and scared no doubt, but persistently human, nonetheless. Human beings were not created to suffer unending abuse. The *imago Dei* will not tolerate it. While I agree with those who characterize the Hamas attack as, in part, an act of terrorism, it was an entirely predictable response to decades of officially sanctioned terrorism systematically meted out by the IDF. This is not to excuse anyone's violence. But it does explain the inevitability of both intifadas and the Hamas attack. What else could Israel expect?

The Israeli journalist Gideon Levy has said these things repeatedly in his columns for the Israeli newspaper *Haaretz*, and he has been savagely maligned for his brave moral clarity:

> Behind all this [the October 7 Hamas attacks] lies Israeli arrogance; the idea that we can do whatever we like, that we'll never pay the price and be punished for it. We'll carry on undisturbed. . . . We'll fire at innocent people, take out people's eyes and smash their faces, expel, confiscate, rob, grab people from their beds, carry out ethnic cleansing and, of course, continue with the unbelievable siege of the Gaza Strip, and everything will be all right.[38]

Israel is learning the hard way that it takes more than a repetitious platitude to make an army moral, and that attempting to sear the consciousness of an entire people is ultimately as dangerous as it is depraved.

38. Levy, *Killing*, 125.

"I've Done Things"

During my first trip to Israel many years ago I scheduled a bus tour of the West Bank with the organization Breaking the Silence (BtS). BtS is an organization made up of IDF veterans whose grieved consciences have moved them to tell the Israeli public the truth about IDF behavior in the occupied territories.[39] Their many published testimonies, both in print and online, are as illuminating as they are heartbreaking.

Toward the end of this tour our bus stopped at the entrance to one of the largest Jewish settlements (illegal according to international law) in the West Bank. Our guide, a former soldier in the IDF, explained the gross disparities in water usage allowed the Jewish settlers in comparison to the severe rationing imposed on the Palestinian population. When he was finished, some on the tour dispersed to take pictures of the lawn sprinklers and water fountains dispersed among the abundance of green lawns.

I hung back and struck up a conversation with our guide. I asked about his own tour of duty with the military. Where had he served? As he began to explain, he quickly started to sob. I learned little about his tour of duty, but I discovered a great deal about his heart.

"I am not a good person," he said as he wept. "I have done things."

I didn't press him to tell me what those "things" had been. But he did tell me that his volunteer work with BtS was a part of his penance, his efforts to make amends for the many immoral things he had done as an IDF soldier.

Here was an expression of genuine morality, not boasting or bragging, but showing itself through confession, repentance, and humble efforts to made amends.

The following excerpts are only a handful taken from the many thousands of testimonies recorded by BtS. They provide a glimpse into the depth of repentance, confession, and restitution that still needs to happen throughout the IDF.

> We took over a central house, set up positions, and one of the sharpshooters identified a man on a roof, two roofs away . . . not armed. I looked at the man through the night vision—he wasn't armed. It was two in the morning. A man without arms, walking on the roof, just walking around. We reported it to the company commander. [He] said "Take him down." [The sharpshooter] fired, took him down. . . . The company commander declared him a

39. See the organization's purpose statement at Breaking the Silence, "Organization."

lookout, meaning he understood that the guy was no threat to us, and he gave the order to kill him and we shot him. . . . To me it's murder. And that's not the only case. We'd laugh about it; we had code names: the lookout, the drummer, the woman, the old man, the boy.[40]

Whenever we would enter houses and there was this scene of the kids hugging the dad or kids who see their dad being taken late at night or their 18-year-old brother, what are they going to grow up to be? Who are they going to want to take revenge on? Us. There's no doubt at all.[41]

Kids would throw stones at us, we'd catch some kid who happened to be there and beat him to a pulp. Even if he didn't throw stones. He would know who did. "Who is it? Who is it?" . . . Let's say we hit him, to put it mildly, until he told us. . . . We went to his [the stone thrower's] house . . . we entered and began to trash the place. . . . We took [the boy] out. We had a commander, never mind his name, who was a bit on the edge. He beat the boy to a pulp, really knocked him around. . . . The commander took a stick, broke it on him boom boom. . . . The commander had no mercy. Really. Anyway, the kid could no longer stand on his feet and was already crying. . . . This was happening every day. These were the little things. And then it becomes a kind of habit. Patrols with beatings happened on a daily basis. We were really going at it. . . . The commander gripped the kid, stuck his gun in his mouth, yelled and all, and the kid was hardly able to walk. We dragged him further, and then he said again: "One more time this kid lifts a stone, anything, I kill him. No mercy."[42]

The Palestinians are constantly subjected to psychological abuse. Just that fact that you can be walking on your street, in your village, in your city, and have the feeling that you are worthless and that any second someone can come and take your things and search you. People have this awareness all the time.[43]

These people [soldiers] don't care. These people view Palestinians as less important or view them as lower class. They [Palestinians]

40. Breaking the Silence, "Death Sentence."
41. Breaking the Silence, "What Is She Going to Become."
42. Breaking the Silence, "Can No Longer Tell Good from Bad."
43. Breaking the Silence, *Military Rule*, 33.

> are dehumanized in the eyes of a lot of individuals that work with the Civil Administration. Like, a complete lack of empathy for Palestinian well-being.[44]

> They [Palestinian boys] play soccer above the post, him and all the kids in the neighborhood. One day, he threw a ball toward the post, not on purpose. The ball just flew in the direction of the post. A border police soldier pulled out his Leatherman [pocket knife] and without saying anything or warning him—punctured the ball. The kid started crying, he came over, took some water, and threw it in the direction of the soldier. Then it got messy. That soldier beat up the kid. Punches, slaps, kicks, pushes, he even dragged him on the ground. The kid got it bad, for real.[45]

> I remember that, at a certain point, we began to break stuff. It's really fun to smash up things, frankly I think it's a fantasy most people cherish. . . . But here, you're 20-years old and you have your chance to do just that, so you start to smash things. I found myself and several others in a moment of this kind of frenzy, breaking tables and doors to bits, scattering a whole bunch of documents in each room, stuff like that. This possibility brings out all the madness in you.[46]

Conclusion

Zionists, both Jewish and Christian, generally work hard at denying that there is anything like "madness" in Israeli society. Christian Zionists commonly seem to assume that as "the chosen people" Jews are intellectually and morally superior to others, that Israel is a morally and culturally superior society. I once heard an evangelical Christian pastor tell his congregation that "the Jews are better than us [gentiles] because they are God's chosen people." For people who are tempted to think this way—even if only a little—it follows that a Jewish military would be the most moral army in the world. This conviction, too, becomes as important an element to Christian Zionist apologetics as it is to Israeli propaganda. As with all propaganda, it eventually becomes an unshakable conviction tragically immune to all evidence to the contrary.

44. Breaking the Silence, *Military Rule*, 70.
45. Breaking the Silence, "Kid Got It Bad."
46. Breaking the Silence, "We Smashed Up Everything."

MYTH #6

The War Against Gaza Is a Just War of Self-Defense

"After running and walking around for about four hours, my friends and I decided to take a break." Natalie Sanandaji, a Jewish American visiting Israel for a well-deserved vacation, was attending the Nova music festival in southern Israel on October 7, 2023. The decision to sit down and rest with her friends at the base of a tall, white tree in the middle of an open field was one of those random, fateful decisions that undoubtedly saved her life.

At 6:30 a.m. that morning Natalie awoke to the sound of rocket fire. A friend encouraged her not to worry. The explosions of intercepted missiles were not an unusual sound in this part of Israel, she was told. Yet soon afterward, festival organizers began shouting for people to flee the sounds of rifle fire in the near distance. Hamas terrorists were rapidly approaching the festival grounds, they were told.

Chaos ensued.

Organizers warned the young people not to congregate around their parked cars, so they scattered in all directions without any sense of where to find safety. Natalie understood that she was running for her life. She and her friends would run in one direction only to be confronted with a mass of people running in the opposite direction, apparently fleeing gunmen as well. How do you run from danger when you don't know where it is?

Throughout the morning Natalie seemed to remain one step ahead of death. Having quickly gone to the restroom, she and her friends ran into a group laying in a ditch. They were tempted to crawl into the culvert themselves, but a friend pointed out that the ditch would become a death trap if it were discovered filled with people. As it happened, after she was rescued, Natalie watched several videos documenting the aftermath of the attack. She saw for herself how close she had come to being murdered, for several videos revealed that both the toilets she briefly entered and the ditch she ran away from had been sprayed with machine gun fire. All the people hiding in both locations were killed.

As Natalie and her friends sat back against the tree trunk trying to catch their breath, they soon noticed a white pickup truck approaching at top speed. Assuming the worst, that the truck was carrying Hamas fighters intent on ending their lives, Natalie and her friends remained seated and waited, surrendering themselves to their fate. There was no chance they could outrun this speeding vehicle.

Sliding to a halt in a cloud of dust, the Jewish driver shouted for them to get into the back. Scrambling into the flatbed as quickly as possible, the entire group was taken to a nearby kibbutz where they were cared for and protected. The anonymous driver made a quick U-turn and drove back toward the festival grounds to rescue more people. Natalie never saw him again. She never learned his name. But he had saved her life.[1]

Many others were not so fortunate. Before the day was over, approximately 1,200 people would be killed; 251 people—men, women, young and old—were kidnapped and taken into Gaza as hostages. The majority have since been returned, dead or alive.

Surveying the Aftermath

Israel's political and military leadership was quick to respond.

On October 9, 2023, Israeli Defense Minister Yoav Gallant declared, "I have ordered a complete siege of the Gaza Strip. There will be no electricity, no food, no fuel, everything is closed. We are fighting human animals, and we are acting accordingly."[2]

As Israeli forces prepared their ground invasion against Gaza's human animals, Prime Minister Benjamin Netanyahu encouraged the soldiers standing now at "the doorstep of the fortress of evil" to "remember what Amalek did to you."[3] The reference to Amalek alluded to an Old Testament story where God commands the Israelites totally to annihilate the Amalekite people (Deut 25:17). Netanyahu went on to short circuit any future

1. Watch Natalie tell her story at NBC News, "American Survivor."
2. Fabian, "Defense Minister Announces," paras. 2–3.
3. Netanyahu, "Statement," October 28, 2023, paras. 2, 4.

criticisms of Israel's behavior insisting that "whoever dares to accuse our soldiers of war crimes are hypocritical liars who lack so much as one drop of morality. The IDF is the most moral army in the world."[4] Netanyahu's "most moral army" was engaging, as he put it, in an epic conflict "of light against darkness." On October 18, 2023, in an address given in Hebrew to the people of Israel, Netanyahu added that "we will not allow humanitarian assistance in the form of food and medicines from our territory to the Gaza Strip."[5] If the Gazan "Amalekites" were not killed by bombs or bullets, they would be starved and allowed to die of their wounds.

Major General Ghassan Alian echoed Gallant and Netanyahu on October 10, 2023, when he made an announcement in Arabic to the people of Gaza. Insisting that the Hamas attack "was not human," he proclaimed that "human animals must be treated as such. There will be no electricity and no water [in Gaza], there will only be destruction. You wanted hell, you will get hell."[6]

Knesset member Nissim Vaturi from the ruling Likud party[7] said that Israel's goal "was erasing the Gaza Strip from the face of the earth." While Israeli Heritage Minister Amichay Eliyahu insisted that there were "no uninvolved civilians" in Gaza, a claim repeated by others many times over in the next two years.[8]

Israel's threats of annihilation against the enemy they dehumanized as barbarians were carried out swiftly, without mercy. The attack began with air strikes that military experts describe as "one of the most intense bombing campaigns in history"; a campaign waged against 2.3 million people, more than half of them children, squeezed into a barricaded concentration camp less than one-quarter the size of greater London, surrounded by machine guns, tanks, and razor wire.[9]

4. Netanyahu, "Statement," October 28, 2023, para. 5.

5. Netanyahu, "Statement," October 18, 2023, para. 5.

6. Pacchiani, "COGAT Chief," paras. 2–3.

7. Likud is Israel's conservative political party descended from the early Revisionist party led by Ze'ev Jabotinsky.

8. Goldenberg, "Harsh Israeli," para. 10. For an extensive list of additional examples that include dehumanizing language inciting genocidal revenge against Gaza, see South Africa's brief against Israel brought before the International Court of Justice, "Application of the Convention," 140–56; also see B'Tselem, *Our Genocide*, 65–70; Shlaim, *Gaza*, 286–96.

9. Shlaim, *Gaza*, 296–97.

Historian Avi Shlaim explains that "in the first week alone, Israel dropped more bombs on Gaza than the US did in Afghanistan each *year* between 2008 and 2019."[10] Israel was carpet bombing the Gaza Strip, dropping more than seventy thousand tons of explosives by June 2024—more tonnage than all the bombs dropped on London, Dresden, and Hamburg throughout all of World War II.[11]

By the end of July 2025, the Palestinian death toll was estimated, conservatively, at more than 60,000 people, with another 145,870 wounded, more than half of the victims being women and children.[12] An additional 147 people have died of starvation now that famine has engulfed the area, thanks to the complete destruction of all Gazan infrastructure and Israel's withholding of humanitarian aid.[13] Between April and mid-July 2025, more than 20,000 children sought treatment for severe malnutrition; more than 3,000 were severely malnourished.[14] Euro-Med Human Rights Monitor places the estimates even higher. According to them, the death toll stands at over 70,300. Who knows the number of uncounted dead still hidden in the tons of piled rubble. Over 150,000 have been injured, and no one has kept track of the numbers of people who have died from their wounds due to the lack of medicine and other medical supplies. Nine out of every ten people killed were civilians, including 117 civil defense workers, 234 journalists, and 1,589 health care professionals.[15] Over forty-three thousand children have been made orphans, many without any living family members remaining. For them a new acronym was created: WCNSF, meaning Wounded Child, No Surviving Family.[16]

A Just War?

Israel achieved at least one of its goals in Gaza. In retaliation for the Hamas attacks on October 7, Israel's political and military leaders vowed to make

10. Shlaim, *Genocide*, 297.

11. Shlaim, *Genocide*, 297; see 298–302 for more on the apocalyptic levels of destruction.

12. Shurafa and Magdy, "Over 60,000."

13. Al Jazeera, "Death Toll"; OCHA, "Considerations for the Delivery"; Jones, "Israel Has Deliberately Starved."

14. Al Jazeera, "Death Toll."

15. Euro-Med, "Infographic."

16. Haidar, "Wounded Child."

Gaza uninhabitable, and that goal has been accomplished. Covered in the gray dust of pulverized cement and concrete, people in the Gaza Strip, brought to the brink of annihilation by the Israeli military, now struggle to survive in a post-apocalyptic moonscape.

Many in the world community have followed South Africa's lead in accusing Israel of committing genocide. Most Israelis, however, insist that they have only fought a just war of self-defense, necessary in the face of imminent extermination, avoiding a near "second holocaust" at the hands of Hamas.[17] But the outcome of this conflict has certainly proven how far-fetched it is to imagine anything like an Hamas-led holocaust. Although Israel has not been able to destroy Hamas outright, Israel's military capabilities have kept Hamas at bay—whatever Hamas's strategic intentions had been in the run-up to October 7. We have yet to consider the validity of Israel's claim to be fighting a just war of self-defense. Doing so requires breaking that claim down into its constituent parts. First, what makes for a just war? And second, what constitutes self-defense?

There is a widespread, mistaken belief that all wars of self-defense are by definition "just." However, a genuinely just war requires more than a defensive posture on one side of the conflict.[18] Space prevents us from examining the just war tradition in detail, for answering the question of morality in warfare requires an analysis of three sets of complex issues (typically designated in Latin): the morality of going to war in the first place (*jus ad bellum*); moral conduct and fighting methods used during the war (*jus in bello*); and the ethics of ending a war and maintaining a just, secure peace (*jus post bellum*). Here, for the sake of space, I will offer an introductory look at only two criteria relevant to both the ethics of going to war (*jus ad bellum*) and ethical practices in combat (*jus in bello*). Those criteria are *discrimination* and *proportionality*. Both criteria are defined by international humanitarian law, especially in the Geneva Convention, Protocol I. Even though Israel still refuses to sign this protocol, its claim to possess the most moral army in the world nonetheless invites a comparison between IDF conduct in Gaza and the broadly accepted standards of international law.

The rule of discrimination—that is, the necessity of distinguishing between civilians and armed combatants, and then exempting civilians from attack—was already touched upon briefly in chapter 5. The imperative of

17. Ferguson, "Hamas"; Shaw, "Uses."

18. For an introduction to the just war tradition, see Bell, *Just War*; Patterson, *Basic Guide*.

protecting civilian life during warfare is highlighted in parts 3 and 4 of Protocol I of the Geneva Convention. Article 35 begins by warning all sides in a conflict that their "right . . . to choose methods or means of warfare is not unlimited" (article 35.1). This limitation is binding on all parties, including those who say they are fighting in self-defense. All sides must avoid methods of warfare that could "cause superfluous injury or unnecessary suffering" (article 35.2), especially to civilians. The fact that a civilian population may include combatants "does not deprive the population of its civilian character" (article 50.3). In other words, the fact that armed fighters are hiding among a civilian population does not justify attacks against the entire population; you can't bomb a school to kill the gunman hiding among the students. That kind of behavior is always illegal because the civilian status of the group is not annulled by the presence of scattered combatants. Attacking such combatants requires more discriminating methods than bombing, putting at risk the civilians making up the vast majority of a group. Complaining that the fighters are using the surrounding crowds as human shields cannot justify killing the "shields" indiscriminately along with the combatants.

Under "Precautionary Measures" Protocol I warns combatants that "constant care shall be taken to spare the civilian population, civilians and civilian objects" (article 57.1). Combatants must "take all feasible precautions" to avoid, or at least to minimize, "incidental loss of civilian life" and damage to civilian property (article 57.2.a). Clearly the Geneva Convention protocols require that military forces must take extreme measures to avoid civilian casualties. This should be the prime directive in warfare—*don't kill civilians*. It seems a fair interpretation of the rules of the Geneva Convention that it should be "illegal" for the IDF to bomb a Gazan apartment complex when its military objective was to remove a single Hamas commander from the conflict. But this is exactly what the IDF has done repeatedly (see below).

Though often stated in absolute terms, the discriminating priorities of civilian protection are nevertheless subject to the calculations of a second criterion: proportionality. This criterion introduces a considerable measure of subjectivity into the equation of restraint—and that ambiguity has given the illusion of moral cover to many of the IDF's most egregious abuses. Protocol I states that attacks are allowed to cause "incidental" loss of civilian life and property *as long as* the damage is not "excessive in relation to the concrete and direct military advantage anticipated" (article 51.5.b and article 57.2.b). In other words, the rule of proportionality requires military planners to conduct a cost-benefit analysis balancing the strategic value of a military objective against the cumulative value of the civilian lives (notice, *not* military personnel) potentially killed during the operation. This is not a simple one-to-one, quantitative calculation. It's not about simply having no more civilian dead than military dead. Rather, it includes murky estimates of the value of human lives over and against the tactical value of an operation. For example, given the estimated military value of such-and-such an objective (capturing a building, destroying a gun emplacement, killing a particular enemy commander), how many civilian deaths might a commander deem acceptable before the inherent value of innocent life outweighs the strategic value of that military objective? This calculation begs several questions. What is the value of civilian life? When are civilian deaths "incidental," and when do they become "excessive"? How are these competing values of human life and military advantage measured? Given the fact that different people will certainly reach different decisions, who gets to make the final calculation and what are their qualifications?

In a following section we will look at the wide latitude as applied in these highly subjective IDF calculations of discrimination and proportionality. Only after examining this real-world evidence can we come to an informed conclusion about whether Israel's behavior in Gaza has been "just."

A War of Self-Defense?

We have seen in the previous section that claiming self-defense does not, in and of itself, justify a no-holds-barred military attack against an opponent. There is no doubt that Hamas committed numerous war crimes on October 7 insofar as hundreds of civilians were killed, wounded, assaulted, and kidnapped as hostages. The slogan that "Israel has a right to defend itself" in the aftermath of such atrocities has been repeated many times since October 7.

However, many Zionists in Israel and elsewhere do not engage with the history of the belligerent and violent Israeli occupation of Gaza prior to October 7. If we are to understand the events of October 7 and the carnage unleashed on Gaza since then, it is important to recognize that this attack is part and parcel of a much larger history. The current conflict is only the latest chapter in a story that goes back at least to 1948 when Zionist military forces drove the Palestinians living in what is now southern Israel out of their home villages into the refugee camps of Gaza.[19] The ethnic cleansing of Palestinians in 1948—known as the Nakba, when three-quarters of a million Palestinians lost their homes and were made refugees during Israel's "war for independence"—was followed by the Six-Day War in 1967 where Israel captured the Gaza Strip and the West Bank, taking control of the refugee population.[20]

Israel prefers to call this land the "disputed" rather than "occupied" territory. As with many nations seeking to obscure actions likely to receive international condemnation, Israel is adept in the use of tools of propaganda. In terms of international law, Israel remains nonetheless an occupier. Israel justifies holding these territories by arguing that Gaza and the West Bank had been illegally annexed by Egypt and Jordan, respectively, prior to their capture by Israel in 1948 and 1967. Arguing that neither territory was, therefore, under the legal sovereignty of a state, since both had been annexed illegally, neither territory may now be considered occupied by a hostile power. Their status continues to be disputed and therefore international anti-occupation law does not apply, at least according to Israel.[21]

Israel's evasive approach to self-defense by means of verbal obscurity is a strategy commonly referred to as *lawfare*: that is, the manipulation of law to avoid its stated intent.[22] If warfare is the continuation of politics by other means, as was claimed by the German military theorist Carl von Clausewitz, then lawfare is the continuation of warfare by other means. However, Israel's stratagems to redefine the issues in order to evade legal culpability while continuing hostilities undeterred cannot erase the plain sense of international law. The second Hague Convention on the Laws and Customs of War on Land clearly states, "Territory is considered occupied when it is actually placed under the authority of the hostile army."[23] The

19. We could trace the beginning of this conflict as far back as 1922 when the League of Nations placed Palestine under the control of a British Mandate that was focused on establishing a Jewish state in Palestinian territory.

20. See Pappé, *Ethnic Cleansing*, 193–95; for more on the Six-Day War, see Louis and Shlaim, *1967*.

21. See the discussion in Quigley, *Case*, 173, 178.

22. Halper, "How Israel Undermines." Ironically, Israel regularly accuses Palestinian representatives of practicing lawfare when they accuse Israel of violating international law. It is a classic instance of an accusation serving as a confession; for further discussion of lawfare, see Erakat, *Justice for Some*, 9–11.

23. The Hague Conventions were written in 1899 and 1907. They were the first major attempts to codify international law governing land warfare. See The Hague Conventions, "Convention (II)," art. 42.

Hague Convention's disinterest in the pre-conquest status of the occupied territory indicates that the answer to that question is irrelevant to the issue of belligerent occupation. Regardless of their previous status, both Gaza and the West Bank have remained "under the authority" of the IDF, "the hostile army," since they were first captured in 1967.[24] This fact is plain for all those who have eyes to see and ears to hear.

UN Resolution 242 emphasizes "the inadmissibility of the acquisition of territory by war."[25] Resolution 2625 (XXV) reiterates that "no territorial acquisition resulting from the threat or use of force shall be recognized as legal."[26] A decade after Israel's occupation had begun, the UN reaffirmed Resolution 242 by codifying Resolution 32/20 condemning Israel's "illegal occupation," reaffirming that "the acquisition of territory by force is inadmissible and that all territories thus occupied must be returned."[27] It does not matter who did or did not have control over captured territory prior to its conquest. The plain sense of international law is clear as articulated by the UN and other legal bodies: The West Bank and Gaza are illegally occupied territories.

Israel has maintained effective military control over the Gaza Strip despite Israel's withdrawal from the Gaza interior in 2005. The IDF withdrawal did not mean an abandonment of military control over Gaza. Prison guards need not live among the prisoners they guard in order to control a prison population; managing the security system is sufficient. Similarly, Israel has always maintained complete control over Gaza's security system, determining who and what may enter and exit Gaza, going so far as to ban such innocuous items as spices, pasta, jam, printing paper, newspapers, notebooks, pens, pencils, fishing ropes, and baby chicks.[28] Israel controls the population registry, the airspace, and the entire militarized border, including the coastline. All of this makes for an effective, ongoing military occupation.

24. See Crump, *Like Birds in a Cage*; Hajjar, "Is Gaza Still Occupied."

25. United Nations Security Council, "Resolution 242."

26. United Nations General Assembly, "Declaration."

27. See United Nations General Assembly, "Situation in the Middle East"; and United Nations Security Council, "Resolution 2334 (2016)," which lists ten resolutions repeating this claim prior to 2016. In 2023 the UN Committee on the Exercise of the Inalienable Rights of the Palestinian People issued the study "The Legality of the Israeli Occupation," which thoroughly describes the legal history of Israel's illegal occupation. See United Nations, *Legality*.

28. Bayoumi and Chalabi, "Toys, Spices."

Occupied People Have a Right to Resist Their Occupation

According to the Geneva Convention, an occupied people has the legal right to enter into "armed conflict" as they "fight against colonial domination and alien occupation and against racist regimes in the exercise of their right of self-determination" (article 1.4). UN Resolution 3236 (XXIX) on "The Question of Palestine" affirms this right of armed resistance by recognizing "the right of the Palestinian people to regain its rights *by all means*" (emphasis mine).[29] UN Resolution 34/29 is titled "Right of the Palestinian people to self-determination." It reiterates the Palestinian right to resistance and to self-defense, not only because their occupation by Israel is illegal but because it "undermines the possibility of the Palestinian people realizing their right to self-determination."[30]

An occupied population has the right to take up arms to fight against its occupiers and to pursue its right to self-determination. Such freedom fighters must obey international law, but there is no need to acquiesce pacifically under belligerent occupation while waiting for others to rectify the injustice. Think of the brave underground fighters who resisted Nazi occupation in France, the Netherlands, and elsewhere across Europe. These men and women are now heroes in the annals of World War II history because they fought for their freedom against belligerent occupation by a brutal, conquering power. The relationship between Israel and the people of Gaza and the West Bank is similar. Whatever Israel's arguments, the Palestinian people are occupied, and for many decades Israel has been the occupier using disproportionate and brutal force to keep Palestinians subservient.

No one has the right to commit war crimes, neither Hamas nor Israel. But armed resistance alone does not make Palestinian fighters into terrorists. Armed resistance is a product of this illegal occupation and consequent subjugation by their occupiers. This is the root of the conflict that Israel and its supporters do not want to address. At the root of the terrible attack launched on October 7, 2023, lies the fundamental question of why. Why do Palestinians continue to fight against the IDF? Why did this violent attack erupt as it did? The answer to such questions must be traced back to the root cause—Israel's occupation. There really is no long-term, just solution that doesn't make way for ending the Israeli occupation of Palestine.

29. United Nations General Assembly, "Question of Palestine."

30. United Nations General Assembly, "Right of the Palestinian People," point 3.

The Occupying Power Does Not Have the Right to Defend Itself

The legal evidence presented thus far has established two points: Israel's ongoing, belligerent, military occupation of the West Bank and Gaza is illegal under international law; and the people living in the West Bank and Gaza have the legal right to resist their occupation and to pursue their own self-determination, even by using force. The logical outcome of these positions is straightforward: *the occupier cannot claim self-defense when it uses violence against the occupied's self-defense.* No party can have the "right" to defend an illegal occupation when the local population resists and fights back, which is what Israel is doing when it fights against Palestinians resisting their occupiers in occupied territory.

Imagine a woman who injures her rapist while defending herself against his assault. Afterward he takes her to court and sues her for breaking his arm when he held it up to defend himself against her kicking and screaming. For this woman to be found guilty of assaulting her assailant while defending herself against rape would be a most perverse injustice, for *an assailant's self-defense cannot supersede the victim's self-defense.* The proper response to a victim's self-defense is to stop the attack she is defending herself against. The same is true of Israel's relationship to the West Bank and Gaza. In the words of Noura Erakat, professor of international law at Rutgers University:

> An occupying power cannot justify military force as self-defense in territory for which it is responsible as the occupant. The problem is that Israel has never regulated its own behavior in the West Bank and Gaza as in accordance with Occupation Law.[31]

Ralph Wilde, professor of international law at the University of London, concurs with Professor Erakat's assessment of the Palestinian situation:

> People within the territory Israel occupies . . . have a right of resistance because of that occupation. A state cannot use force illegally, precipitating resistance, and then claim it has a right to defend itself against that resistance, even when that resistance goes beyond what is lawful.[32]

31. Erakat, "No, Israel Does Not," para. 11; Erakat, *Justice for Some*, 179, "colonized peoples have the right to use force in pursuit of their self-determination"; also 189–90.

32. Wilde, "Israel's War," para. 16; also Wilde, "International Law."

Israel continues to use illegal force against Palestinians as long as it continues to occupy Gaza and the West Bank. The Hamas-led attack on October 7 was a particularly violent act of resistance against that ongoing, illegal occupation. Except for the war crimes that were committed—note, that Israeli soldiers were targeted by Hamas on October 7, while upsetting, is not a war crime—the Hamas attack was legal and permissible according to international humanitarian law. *We see, therefore, that Israel's unspeakably savage assault against the people of Gaza, together with its expansive attacks throughout the West Bank, are not acts of self-defense.* Quite the opposite. Israel's attack on Gaza is a particularly brutal continuation of the many war crimes Israel has continued to perpetrate against the Gazan people since 1948.

The Dahiya Doctrine and Just War

The Dahiya Doctrine arose out of Israel's thirty-four-day war against Lebanon in 2006. At that time the Dahiya suburb of southern Beirut housed the Hezbollah headquarters. In its efforts to eradicate Hezbollah by decapitating its leadership, Dahiya was flattened by Israel's indiscriminate bombarding, killing nearly one thousand civilians, about a third of them children.[33] This practice of using indiscriminate, disproportionate force had a long history in Israeli tactics, going back as far as the guerrilla raids led by Orde Wingate; it then proliferated during the numerous massacres committed by Israel in the 1947–1949 war. But it became a well-defined strategy in the second Lebanon war with a specific label: the Dahiya Doctrine.

General Gade Eizenkot, who led the attacks throughout this war, finally revealed the existence of this doctrine in 2008. During an interview with *Reuters*, he explained:

> What happened in the Dahiya quarter of Beirut in 2006 will happen in every village from which Israel is fired on. . . . We will apply disproportionate force . . . and cause great damage and destruction there. From our standpoint, these are not civilian villages, they are military bases. . . . This is not a recommendation. This is a plan. And it has been approved.[34]

33. Institute for Middle East Understanding, "Explainer"; 121 IDF soldiers were killed by Hezbollah.

34. Reuters, "Israel Warns," paras. 2, 4–5; see Hajjar, "Israel as Innovator," 43.

Israel readily admits that its military campaigns against Gaza in 2008, 2012, and 2014 were all guided by the principles of the Dahiya Doctrine; that is, the application of overwhelming, indiscriminate, disproportionate use of force, the goal of which is to inflict immense destruction without regard to the difference between civilian and military targets.[35] When non-state actors behave this way, they are rightly called terrorists. When a nation-state behaves in an identical manner, the only appropriate way to describe its behavior is to call such a nation a terrorist state. Thus, Israel is using its massive, high-tech arsenal, largely supplied by the United States, to deploy terrorist tactics against the people of Gaza. Why should excessive and indiscriminate killings amount to terrorism only if perpetuated by non-state actors? Continuing to apply the Dahiya Doctrine makes for the very antithesis of a just war, no matter the spark that started the latest conflagration. I surmise that according to its own military doctrine, Israel is a terrorist state flagrantly violating international humanitarian law.

When Artificial Intelligence Applies the Dahiya Doctrine

Israel's war against Gaza has relied heavily on the use of artificial intelligence (AI) for the selection of military targets, including the identification of individual actors in need of elimination. One could be forgiven for imagining that military applications of AI would lead to a reduction in civilian casualties during a bombing campaign. Surely the use of AI targeting systems would bring increased precision and lower casualties to the battlefield. This has not been the case, however—at least, not in the ways that one would expect. During Israel's assault on Gaza, record numbers of civilian deaths, far exceeding those of militants, has proven to be the norm. This, despite the objections of Israel's defenders—such as John Spencer who insists that Israel has taken unprecedented measures to minimize civilian casualties.[36] Such arguments ring as hollow as the IDF claims to be the most moral army in the world. Neither claim holds up to any scrutiny. As we will see, Israel's own military leaders have refuted the claims of Israel's defenders as they readily admit that the IDF's use of AI has all but tossed the laws

35. Marei, "Dahiya Doctrine," 75.

36. Spencer, "Israel Implemented." For convincing critiques of Spencer's pro-Israel apologetics, see Bryant, "We Must Face"; L. Lewis, "Israeli Civilian Harm"; Spagat, "Netanyahu Got It Wrong."

of discrimination and proportionality out the window. As one IDF intelligence officer confessed to journalists from *The Guardian*, when choosing the next bombing target "in practice, the proportionality criterion did not exist."[37] Adhering to the laws of proportionality will inevitably suffer once an army decides to increase its dependence on dumb bombs (munitions lacking guidance systems) and to "significantly expand" the bombing of targets that are "not distinctly military in nature,"[38] including private residences, public buildings like schools and hospitals, high-rise apartment blocks, and all infrastructure. Israel has attacked all such targets.

Israel's principal AI programs tasked with identifying Hamas targets are called "Lavender," "The Gospel," and "Where's Daddy?" By tracking cell phone locations, including daily patterns of movement, frequent stopping places, and regular personal associations, these programs identify both the places and the people judged to have connections with Hamas militants. The programs generate thousands of potential targets nearly instantaneously every day, depending on how widely or narrowly the data parameters are set.[39] At one stage early in the Gaza campaign, Lavender had identified thirty-seven thousand potential targets with fierce pressure to find even more targets coming from officers higher in the chain of command.[40] It is not surprising then that military sources reported that "damage to civilians is the real purpose" of these AI generated attacks.[41]

A survey of the investigative reports that have been published about Israel's use of AI programs demonstrates that IDF reliance on these computer tools increased over time because they could produce greater results in terms of faster, easier, and cheaper targeting.[42] Human calculation was taken out of the equation. Killing efficiency, not accuracy, was the concern. The emphasis was on quantity not on quality.[43] Israel has been using Gaza to chart new horizons in industrialized, mechanized warfare. With fewer man-hours invested, AI targeting can kill more people, more easily, more quickly, for less money. One intelligence officer confessed that the

37. McKernan and Davies, "Machine," para. 40.

38. Abraham, "Mass Assassination," para. 3.

39. No one outside of the IDF knows exactly how the programming occurs.

40. McKernan and Davies, "Machine."

41. Abraham, "Mass Assassination," para. 35.

42. This comes across very clearly in Abraham, "Lavender"; Abraham, "Mass Assassination"; McKernan and Davies, "Machine."

43. Abraham, "Mass Assassination."

calculations for permissible collateral damage (i.e., civilian casualties) was "so permissive that it had an element of revenge."[44] There was a sliding scale for deciding the allowable number of civilians that could be killed when targeting different ranks of Hamas commanders. For a Hamas brigade commander, for instance, the IDF was "willing to kill hundreds of civilians," whereas only a dozen or fewer might be allowed for a lower-level operative.[45]

One outstanding example of such bloody-minded calculation was surely Israel's attack on the Nuseirat refugee camp on June 8, 2024, in order to rescue four hostages.[46] In that rescue operation, Israel managed to kill 274 civilians with another 698 bystanders injured. The nearby hospital in Deir al-Balah was overwhelmed with corpses and the wounded. Israeli General Irzhak Brik, whose forces rescued the hostages, described his team's actions as a "surgical" operation that was driven by "values."[47] As we have seen, most certainly, the values the general referred to are those self-justifying values held by the most moral army in the world (see chapter 5). Similarly, the operation almost certainly remained "surgical" because the 972 casualties fell within the predetermined AI parameters permitted for collateral damage during this operation. This is certainly not what the authors of the Geneva Convention had in mind when they defined the principle of proportionality in terms of "incidental" civilian casualties. Today's political Zionism uses a cold calculus, even programmed into the bloody parameters of their custom AI targeting software that justifies the greater value of four Jewish lives over that of nearly one thousand maimed and murdered Palestinians. This is as surgical as removing a leg for an ingrown toenail.

Perhaps the most shocking of these program applications is the IDF's reliance on "Where's Daddy?" to target individual suspects in their homes. The program's viciously cynical name gives the game away. It is much easier to target suspected Hamas members when they are at home, eating or sleeping with their families. The mockingly titled program "Where's Daddy?" identifies these targets, most often after dark, allowing the entire family and their neighbors to be killed with a single strike.[48] This is easily

44. Abraham, "Lavender," para. 86.

45. Abraham, "Lavender," para. 86.

46. See Gideon Levy's discussion of this operation in *Killing*, 287–89.

47. Levy, *Killing*, 288.

48. Abraham, "Mass Assassination."

done since, as was confessed by Israeli air force Chief of Staff Omer Tishler, the army's "roof-knocking policy" is no longer used when it is believed that there is an enemy in the house.[49] The target's family, friends, and neighbors are never given the opportunity to flee since they are only disturbed by the bomb that kills and maims them. "Where's Daddy?" is obviously another factor in the high civilian casualty rate all throughout Gaza; it certainly does not cohere with the claims of Israel's defenders that the IDF takes extraordinary measures to avoid killing civilians. In fact, Israel is knowingly, deliberately killing hundreds of civilians every day and night, without apology or hesitation.

Fourteen months into Israel's attack on Gaza *The New York Times*, which normally remains a stalwart defender of Israel's behavior,[50] published a major article titled "Israel Loosened Its Rules to Bomb Hamas Fighters, Killing Many More Civilians." Interviewing one hundred soldiers and officials, including twenty-five who worked directly with monitoring the different AI programs, the investigative journalists also reveal the shockingly permissive approach to discrimination and proportionality adopted by the IDF. Learning that numerous bombing missions were approved which directly threatened to kill over one hundred civilians each as collateral damage, the *Times* concludes that Israel has "crossed an extraordinary threshold for a contemporary Western military."[51]

Successfully targeting senior Hamas commander Ibrahim Biari included obliterating at least 125 others living in his building.

When an Israeli fighter jet bombed Mr. Shaldan al-Najjar on October 10, 2023, the explosion killed not only its intended target but also al-Najjar's stepmother, four children, a younger brother, a sister-in-law, and thirteen nephews and nieces, including a two-month-old baby boy.

Such human slaughter is the very opposite of what is normally conveyed by the words "precision" (strikes), "surgical" (attacks), or "incidental" (civilian casualties). Israel is repetitiously swinging a vast scythe through the human grain field that is Gaza, harvesting Palestinian lives as if they had been planted only for destruction.

49. Abraham, "Mass Assassination," para. 47. Roof knocking involves sending a smaller missile lacking an explosive nose device to hit the roof of a building before the live bombs or missiles are dropped. The idea is that the non-explosive impact will warn the residents to leave their building before it is bombed. Of course, this assumes that everyone in the building is mobile and that they are all able to hear the "knock" on the roof.

50. See Shupak, *Wrong Story*, 41–46, 51, 54, 103–9.

51. Kingsley et al., "Israel Loosened," para. 14.

General Tishler's confession about roof knockings has additional significance when it is pondered for a moment. Israel's roof-knocking policy allowed for the dropping of dummy bombs with no explosive heads mounted on them onto the roofs of targeted buildings. The purpose was to give civilians opportunity to escape unharmed before the live bombs were dropped. But let's think about this general's confession for a moment. If the army now only knocks on the roofs of buildings the IDF knows do not harbor Hamas targets, then they are obviously bombing buildings for the sake of bombing buildings while knowingly risking civilian lives. There can be no other purpose than the complete demolition of Gaza.

"Nothing happens by accident," says one IDF intelligence officer:

> When a 3-year-old girl is killed in a home in Gaza, it's because someone in the army decided it wasn't a big deal for her to be killed—that it was a price worth paying in order to hit [another] target. We are not Hamas. These are not random rockets. Everything is intentional. We know exactly how much collateral damage there is in every home.[52]

The unreflective irony in this IDF officer's boast about "not being Hamas" is bone-chilling. Hamas periodically fires unguided, primitive missiles into Israel which injure remarkably few Israelis. The IDF on the other hand drops tons of massive bombs on Gazans—so far, the equivalent destructive power of the nuclear bombs dropped on Hiroshima and Nagasaki—knowing perfectly well that an innumerable number of innocent civilians will be killed. In fact, they know specifically which civilians will be victimized. But because this Israeli carnage is not random but targeted, it becomes moral and acceptable even though it flagrantly violates international law? Really? Is intentionally, knowingly killing a three-year-old girl any less horrific than killing her unknowingly? No, it is not. By my calculation it is more horrific.

Conclusion

By every possible measure, the last thing anyone can honestly say about Israel's assault against Gaza is that it is a just war of self-defense. It is actually a most unjust war of aggressive revenge. Unfortunately, those pro-Israel advocates who continue to deny that a genocide has taken place in

52. Abraham, "Mass Assassination," para. 7.

Gaza merely reveal that they, too, remain blinded by the dastardly effects of Israeli propaganda. The evidence is overwhelming: Israeli military planners show no actual regard for the value of Palestinian life. Military commanders admit that the humanitarian constraints of proportionality and discrimination are functionally irrelevant to IDF strategy.

We also see the importance of historical perspective in determining whether or not the assault on Gaza has been a war of self-defense. Recognizing Israel as a settler-colonial state that has always sought to eliminate Palestinians from the land, replacing them with Jewish colonizers, makes it impossible to excuse Israel's actions as defensive. Since at least 1947, and even earlier, the Palestinians have been defending themselves against Zionist aggression and attempts at ethnic cleansing. International law is clear—Palestinians have a right to fight back against their Zionist occupiers. Whereas Israel has no right to tighten its grip on occupied territory or to eliminate those fighters who continue to resist their illegal occupation. Yes, Palestinians fighters committed war crimes on October 7, just as Israeli fighters have committed innumerable war crimes in their colonization of Palestine. In an ideal world, all war crimes would be investigated and prosecuted with equal vigor. No one would be excused because of their superior political influence or more effective propaganda campaign.

CONCLUSIONS

Truth, Morality, and the Kingdom of God

All governments lie. At least that was the professional opinion of the well-known American investigative journalist I. F. Stone.[1] And I am convinced that Stone was correct. All governments lie because all governments are invested in curating their national mythologies by spreading the self-justifying propaganda that bolsters their mythological national image. Thus, the US government lies. The Israeli government lies.

However, there is also a theological reason for the consistent lies of nationalistic propaganda. All governments lie, whether by commission or omission, because all governments are created, organized, operated, and applauded by imperfect human beings who have a tendency, at times, to lie themselves. Just as flawed components will produce a flawed product, so seriously flawed human beings will produce seriously flawed governments.

I happen to be a firm believer in the Christian doctrine of original sin according to which everyone, without exception, whether we realize it or not, whether we admit to it or not, is inclined toward walking away from their Creator and going their own way to "do their own thing." When left to ourselves we tend to seek our own good rather than the good of others, and when we make a mistake our first instinct is to cover our tracks so that no one will know that we had anything to do with the mess we left behind. Of course, human beings are complex. We are not simply evil all the time. Far from it. Being made as the image of God, as I believe we all are, also enables human beings to accomplish great and beautiful things, to display amazing mercy, and to make tremendous sacrifices for the things we know to be true. Yet, the specter of our human foibles, our numerous, unshakable imperfections continually haunt our every move, whether with temptations

1. See MacPherson, *All Governments Lie!*

to moral regression or actual duplicity known only to ourselves. Each of us harbors a Dr. Jekyll as well as a Mr. Hyde.

The only ruler who has never lied or dissembled about his government's policies—such things as loving God with our whole selves and loving our neighbor as ourselves—is Jesus Christ, the crucified King of kings. The kingdom of God is the only realm where truthfulness and honesty are not only modeled perfectly by the ruler in charge but are insisted upon as the universal standard for every kingdom citizen. Kingdom citizens will want nothing to do with falsehood of any kind, whether it be personal distortions, corporate duplicity, or the nationalistic propaganda of a boastful nation-state. Loyalty to the kingdom of God means that the nationalistic, quasi-religious ties of loyalty, forged by every nation-state with its citizenry, will (ideally) have little to no power over us. If I am secure in knowing that my true citizenship makes me a child of God in the kingdom of God, then my heart, mind, and conscience are free to question every political status quo, to investigate every nationalistic claim to exceptionalism, to reject every patriotic message that demonizes the "enemy," to disavow every loyalty that competes for my faithfulness to God's standards, to dismiss every national mythology, and finally to jettison every conviction, no matter how firm, that has failed to measure up to God's requirements of loving my enemy with humility and grace.

None of this is easy, and there are many impostors along life's way that will seek to deceive us outright or to confuse their own ideologies with loyalty to God's kingdom. I am convinced that Zionism is one of these deceptive ideologies that eagerly distorts faithfulness to Jesus Christ by infusing territorial, ethnic, and nationalistic commitments into the Christian church's approach to kingdom living. Christian Zionist propaganda would have us believe that the modern Israeli nation-state is fulfilling a unique role in salvation-history on which all of God's final promises ultimately depend. Israel is a perpetually victimized nation, forever innocent and always victorious because it is a chosen people, even as it is persecuted by worldwide antisemitism. This mythology tells us to believe that blessing Israel through our prayers, finances, and wholehearted personal support is the most direct way to secure God's blessings in our own lives. Yet, the discerning kingdom citizen will shed these pieces of Zionist mythology and never forget that all such ideological intrusions are idolatrous compromises with a very different way of living. There is no sacred geography (see chapters 1 and 2) for God's people this side of the new heavens and the new earth.

The doors to the kingdom of God remain open for all races and ethnicities without prejudice; none are more special to God than any others, regardless of the Zionist belief in Israel's chosenness. There is one and the same avenue to eternal life for all people everywhere. There is one invitation into the family of God, and as Paul, a Jewish apostle, said to a gentile church, "There is neither Greek nor Jew" (Gal 3:28). For Christians, the door is open to all, without precondition, and without undo external burdens. Jesus, our Jewish Messiah, fulfills all such demands and embraces all peoples in himself equally.

It is important always to continue to grow as a Christian person, not to mention as a maturing adult. For this to happen, it's essential to have an openness to investigate all sides of a debate. Will I honestly engage the evidence offered by my ideological opponent, or am I too fearful to read, analyze, and thoughtfully consider the arguments presented by the other side? As a young graduate student, I quickly learned how important it is to understand the arguments promoting positions I disagreed with just as thoroughly as I grasped those bolstering my own preferred views. At times this research led me to change my mind and adopt a new position. I hope and pray that having read this book my Zionist readers have seen the value of considering the historical alternatives on offer and will go on to do further research on their own. Elsewhere I have told my own story of personal transformation from a young Christian Zionist to the non-Zionist that I am today.[2] It's been a long journey.

The French Christian intellectual Jacques Ellul wrote extensively about the negative consequences of long-term exposure to propaganda in his magisterial work *Propaganda: The Formation of Men's Attitudes*. These consequences should be of concern to us all as I am convinced that Israeli state propaganda has affected Western Christian Zionism almost as much as it has the Israeli public (see the introduction). Ellul observes that one of the most severe negative effects of propaganda is "the suppression of all critical judgment. . . . We are dealing here with one of propaganda's most durable effects."[3] Strengthening one's critical faculties requires studying both sides of an issue, remaining open to new information, and possessing a willingness to change our opinions in light of new evidence. Zionist propaganda works against this transformation process from beginning to end. This fact is difficult to challenge successfully, but it must be said. The totalizing and

2. See Crump, *Like Birds in a Cage*, 1–11.

3. Ellul, *Propaganda*, 170.

solidifying effects of long-term exposure to propaganda can ingrain prejudices, harden biases, affirm "ready-made judgments" that never submit to cross-examination, and confirm the deep-seated "rightness" of one's beliefs by giving them a religious quality. In fact, when propaganda is promoting a religious conviction that serves as a life-ordering, life-affirming mythology—as Christian Zionism does for its adherents[4]—the melding of propaganda's message with personal religious belief becomes indivisible. To be a person of true faith requires embracing propaganda's mythos wholeheartedly. Changing one's mind is akin to religious apostasy; it is not simply a matter of weighing the evidence and making a rational decision. A lengthy citation from Ellul is helpful here:

> To the extent man [*sic*] needs justifications, propaganda provides them. But whereas his ordinary justifications are fragile and may always be open to doubts, those furnished by propaganda are irrefutable and solid. The individual believes them and considers them to be eternal truths. He can throw off all sense of guilt; he loses all feeling for the harm he might do. . . . Propaganda has created in him a system of opinions and tendencies which may not be subjected to criticism. . . . He feels personally attacked when these certainties are attacked. There is a feeling here akin to that of something sacred. And this genuine taboo prevents the individual from entertaining any new ideas that might create ambiguity within him . . . propaganda tends to give a person a religious personality.[5]

I am convinced that Ellul's analysis of propaganda and its negative effects helps to explain the extreme reactions I encounter when I speak to Christian Zionist audiences. Why do men (in particular) shout at me, pound on tables, interrupt my presentations, march out fuming, and come forward afterward to argue? These dubious responses testify to the fact that I am not seeing evidence of Christian disagreement but am witnessing the eruptions of a thoroughly propagandized personality. The piety of Christian faith and the religious sensibilities of Zionist propaganda have fused into one. To question the myths of Zionism is to question Jesus. To follow Jesus is to march boldly in the Zionist mythos parade.

4. See Burge, "Christian Zionism as Mythology."

5. Ellul, *Propaganda*, 165–66.

Propaganda and Kingdom Ethics

All propaganda aims ultimately at changing the way people behave. Influencing public opinion, changing the ways in which a crowd thinks and what they believe is only the beginning of the propaganda process. When all else is said and done, propaganda has not been completely successful until it influences human behavior. But the same can be said for the work of the Holy Spirit in the Christian life. Keeping in step with the Spirit (Gal 5:25) will transform a person's character, which in turn will change the way that person lives. As the apostle Paul reminds us, the fruit of the Spirit is love, joy, peace, patience, gentleness, goodness, faith, meekness, and self-control, all of which describes a radically new, Spirit-filled life whose godly actions will testify to the arrival of God's kingdom on earth. Propaganda, whether Zionist or not, is motivated by an altogether different sort of spirit.

But the power of the gospel to reshape us in conformity with the ways of Christ must confront propaganda's converse power to harden us in the ways of worldly opinion. I believe the story of Frederick Douglass's life in the pre–Civil War South offers a useful analogy for grasping how this confrontation often works itself out. Douglass's autobiography describes his master's conversion to Christian faith at a Methodist camp meeting in 1832. There, Douglass says, his master "experienced religion." This man had always been particularly cruel, and Douglass held out hope that the master's newfound religion would soften his heart, making him "more kind and humane." Perhaps he would even emancipate his slaves. But in fact,

> It neither made him to be humane to his slaves, nor to emancipate them. If it had any effect on his character, it made him more cruel and hateful in all his ways: for I believe him to have been a much worse man after his conversion than before . . . after his conversion, he found religious sanction and support for his slaveholding cruelty.[6]

Later in his story Douglass goes on to generalize his observations saying, "Of all the slaveholders with whom I have ever met, religious slaveholders are the worst. I have ever found them the meanest and basest, the most cruel and cowardly, of all others."[7]

How may we account for this? Why would Christian conviction make such slave owners the harshest of masters?

6. Douglass, *Narrative*, 61.
7. Douglass, *Narrative*, 79.

When it came to the questions of slavery and the dehumanization of black Africans, I think it safe to assume that the men and women of the antebellum South were among the most heavily propagandized people imaginable. Dehumanizing, proslavery messages were ubiquitous, broadcast from the pulpit, Bible studies, Sunday school lessons, newspapers, books, leaflets, theater performances, political debates, and casual conversation. It was a deeply ingrained ideology as widespread and all pervasive as the air people breathed. Because it was the popular opinion of the masses, it was taken for granted that the logic of proslavery arguments were as obvious as the nose on your face, for the religious and the irreligious alike. This all-encompassing proslavery propaganda became the lattice work that sustained the popular mythology of white racial superiority, complete with biblical prooftexts. This myth was as old as time, or at least as old as white European exploration and colonialism.

Now add Christian piety to this social, cultural, mythological stew. Even a superficial reading of the Bible will uncover numerous verses condoning and regulating the institution of slavery.[8] Nowhere is it explicitly condemned; nor does God overtly order its termination as a human institution. When an evangelical fervor for obeying God's word was combined with the commonly accepted mythology of anti-black racism and white supremacy, propagated by the ubiquitous proslavery propaganda found in the deep South, it is not hard to understand how human impulses toward cruelty with slaves (after all, they were subhuman) could become a religious imperative. Through the propaganda process Christian religion was made to cohere with racial mythology. This would especially be the case if the revivalist religion on offer never challenged or rebuked the proslavery status quo. The preacher's silence condoned propaganda's message, serving as tacit approval for the keeping of slaves. Church-going men and women not only kept slaves but disciplined them harshly when they stepped out of line. Thus, the ever-present propaganda reaffirmed the religious value of the racial myth—white people were superior and made to own inferior black people.

My comparison of proslavery propaganda and Zionist propaganda is harsh but apropos. In this comparison the Palestinian people correspond to the abused slaves in the American South. The Jewish citizens of Israel and Christian Zionists everywhere are comparable to the Southern slave owners.

8. See Crump, "Echoes of Slavery"; the most widespread proslavery literature was religious literature.

Both Jewish and Christian Zionists are so heavily propagandized with Zionist mythology that Israel's contemporary state of affairs—condemning its Palestinian citizens to second-class status; living in Jewish-only neighborhoods; segregating its school children into Jewish-only schools; keeping the entire population of Gaza and the West Bank suppressed beneath a draconian military occupation; committing a genocide in Gaza largely accepted and approved by both the Israeli and the evangelical Christian public—seems perfectly normal in a nation-state that labels itself the only democracy in the Middle East. As Ellul warns us, like all propagandized people, Zionists, too, "can throw off all sense of guilt," losing "all feeling for the harm [they] might do."[9] In this world of anti-Arab racism the stories told by the Israeli establishment are always trustworthy, while Palestinian stories are always suspect.

I once was talking with an Israeli woman who worked for a human rights organization called B'Tselem.[10] We were discussing the brutish military "emergency regulations" that the IDF imposes as occupation law over the millions of Palestinian people living in the West Bank. She was explaining to me how the average Israeli goes about her daily life completely immune to the brutal realities occurring in her name only a short distance away in the occupied territories. I asked her how she thought this was possible. How could so many remain so blind and deaf? How can the bulk of an entire society ignore the daily cruelty being perpetrated on its behalf right next door?

"Mass psychosis," she said, shaking her head. "That's all I can think of."

I am now convinced that it is a mass psychosis created by Israeli state propaganda inculcating the myths of political Zionism. The myths were contrived immediately. The myth of Jewish supremacy stretching its legs in a revived Israeli ethnocracy, the Jewish nation-state, activated the earliest waves of Zionist colonizers. The Orientalist myth of Palestinian inferiority and backwardness, a prejudice which justified their marginalization, fit hand in glove with this vision of a Jewish ethnocracy. From the beginning, early Zionist leaders spread the falsehood about Palestine being "an empty land without a people," even though by the late nineteenth century nearly one thousand bustling villages dotted the countryside, and both the coastal

9. Ellul, *Propaganda*, 165.

10. Its full title is B'Tselem: The Israeli Information Center for Human Rights in the Occupied Territory; see www.btselem.org.

plain and interior highlands boasted thriving metropolises.[11] In this book I have examined six additional myths in some detail. They are all myths in the fullest sense of that term: Most fundamentally, they are demonstrably untrue; but more than that, they are all integral pieces of the (Christian) Zionist mythology that is emphasized repeatedly through the Zionist propaganda machines in Israel and American evangelicalism. As (Christian) Zionist mythology, each point is integral to the Zionist worldview infusing, shaping, and securing the personal identity of every Christian Zionist believer—so much so that believing in the myths of Zionism can become part and parcel of believing in Jesus Christ.

Let's recall these myths: Modern Israel is the direct descendent of biblical Israel. The Bible literally predicts Israel's reestablishment in the promised land. The Israel–Palestine conflict is rooted in ancient Arab antisemitism. Israel's victory over the Arab states in 1948 was a miracle. Israel's military is the most moral army in the world. The war against Gaza was a just war of self-defense. These myths form only a few of the rough-hewn, irregular, abrasive planks nailed together in the Zionist platform that eventually works to demean and oppress the Palestinian people. In believing these myths, in allowing our minds and hearts to be shaped by such fallacious propaganda, we follow in the footsteps of Frederick Douglass's evangelical master. In approving of Israel's bloodthirsty slaughter throughout the Gaza Strip, we cheer on the propagandized Christian master whose whip tore strips of flesh from Douglass's backside. In keeping silent about or, worse yet, in keeping ourselves glibly detached from Israel's ongoing crimes against humanity, we join the choir of pious slave-owners who sang "Nothing but the Blood of Jesus" while despoiling their hymnals with their own blood-stained hands. In calling for the American church "to stand with Israel," leaders such as Russell Moore, editor-in-chief of *Christianity Today* magazine,[12] call for evangelicals to stand with the slave trader, to exploit his human cargo, to rip mothers from their children, to tear wives from their husbands, and to perpetuate the dehumanization of brown-skinned people as settler-colonialists have always done.

By the power of the Holy Spirit there is no propaganda message that cannot be broken; there is no mythology whose power cannot be undone. But it requires a devotion to the truth, the truth of Jesus Christ, the truth about the past, and the truth about Israel–Palestine's current state of affairs.

11. Pappé, *Ten Myths*, 6.

12. Moore, "American Christians."

It is time for all of God's people to walk in the power of the Spirit of holiness where the light of God's truth will dispel the darkness of Zionist propaganda. It happened with the abolitionist movement in the past. It can happen again. All those who call themselves disciples of Jesus Christ must choose an honest life of obedience in God's kingdom, while rejecting the lies and inhumanity of Zionist mythology.

Next Steps

I am being blunt because I am calling all those who are flirting with Christian Zionism, all those who are not fully convinced or are still treading on the margins of Zionist mythology, to turn away from that deception and *to deprogram themselves*. The apostle Paul calls us all to stop "conforming to the pattern of this world, but to be transformed by the renewing of your mind." Only then can we recognize the ideas and behaviors that have God's approval (Rom 12:2). Similarly, Paul charges the Corinthians to reject the intellectual standards of this world, understanding that Christians do not fight with worldly weapons (2 Cor 10:2–4). Instead, through the work of the Spirit, "we take captive every thought to make it obedient to Christ" (2 Cor 10:5). The myths of Zionism rebel against Christ and reject the good news of the gospel.

The first steps in this spiritual deprogramming process involve prayer and Bible study. Ask the Lord to renew your heart and mind so that you will grow into the mind of Christ. Christ never approves of mass slaughter, oppression, discrimination, or stripping people of their dignity. Tell the Lord that you want to repent of any ungodly ideologies and thought patterns that do not conform to the ways of Christ. Ask him to show you what those are. Then immerse yourself in the four Gospels, giving special attention to the way Jesus treats people and to the ways he teaches his disciples to treat others. Ask the Father to make you more like Jesus. Respond to God's promptings. Change your behavior accordingly. Ask yourself how such Christ-like behavior and thinking should be applied to Palestinians suffering under military occupation (remember the parable of the Good Samaritan), and to Jewish and Christian Zionists who believe that life in a Jewish ethnocracy,[13] where all non-Jews are discriminated against as second-class citizens, is God's own intended design. Is there some way for you to reach out to Palestinian people living in your community? If so, contact them. Explain

13. See Yiftachel, *Ethnocracy*.

your interest in learning more about their perspectives on Israel–Palestine. Invite them over for dinner and listen to their stories.

Finally, broaden your education. Just as propaganda relies upon information, so also deprogramming requires alternative information. No, this is not a propaganda contest—one set of misleading information battling against another equally misleading set of "facts." No one can honestly make such a judgment until they have first immersed themselves in the alternative storyline. You cannot make an honest judgment in advance. To begin your alternative immersion, therefore, I suggest that you begin with a few autobiographies describing the struggles and the trauma of Palestinian life in Palestine: Alex Awad, *Palestinian Memories: The Story of a Palestinian Mother and Her People*; Elias Chacour, *Blood Brothers*; and Jean Zaru, *Occupied with Nonviolence: A Palestinian Woman Speaks*.

Next, buy three books by the Jewish historian Ilan Pappé.[14] Begin with *A Very Short History of the Israel–Palestine Conflict* (2024). Professor Pappé has devoted his entire career to researching and writing about various aspects of Israel's modern history. He is an expert in his field of study. Learn about his alternative historical narrative from this short introduction. Then move on to another short book, Pappé's topical text *Ten Myths About Israel* (2017). This work has numerous endnotes and citations that you can follow up on in your own investigations. Make note of how many of your own beliefs about Israel–Palestine are being challenged or deconstructed by Professor Pappé as examples of Zionist mythology. Finally, tighten your seat belt and sit down to read Pappé's classic work, *The Ethnic Cleansing of Palestine* (2006). If this book doesn't challenge you and leave you feeling deeply disturbed, then you need to pray harder for the redemption of your conscience. I'm serious.

There are also qualified evangelical Christian authors who offer in-depth critiques of Christian Zionism providing an alternative, biblical perspective on these questions. Here is a short list of recommendations: two books by Dr. Gary M. Burge, *Whose Land? Whose Promise? What Christians Are Not Being Told About Israel and the Palestinians* (2003) and *Jesus and the Land* (2010); two books by Dr. Rob Dalrymple, *These Brothers of Mine: A Biblical Theology of Land and Family and a Response to Christian Zionism* (2015) and *The Land of Contention: Biblical Narratives and the Struggle for*

14. For a more extensive introduction to the issues at stake, the bibliography contains several additional books well worth reading by Colin Chapman, Noura Erakat, Norman Finkelstein, Simha Flapan, Rashid Khalidi, Benny Morris, Michael Palumbo, Edward Said, and Avi Shlaim.

the Holy Land (2024); one book edited by Drs. Bruce N. Fisk and J. Ross Wagner, *Being Christian After the Desolation of Gaza* (2025); and another book by myself, *Like Birds in a Cage: Christian Zionism's Collusion in Israel's Oppression of the Palestinian People* (2023).

Again, I am not asking you to replace one batch of dubious information with another. This is not a matter of personal preference but of a genuine search for the truth about history. Even while remembering that all knowledge about history is relative, we can still affirm that the claims of historical knowledge range from downright false to reasonably trustworthy. On the one hand, we know that George Washington never chopped down a cherry tree; that is a myth, pure and simple.[15] It is on par with the Zionist myth about Palestine being an empty land before European Jewish colonizers began their settlements. On the other hand, everyone agrees that Israel attacked the USS Liberty, a surveillance ship sailing in international waters, on June 8, 1967. Historians and survivors still debate whether the attack was deliberate or an accident, but no one contests the fact that it happened.[16]

Remember that ever since Ben Zion Dinur (1884–1973) was appointed Israel's first minister of education and culture in 1951,[17] the Israeli government has invested great effort in the manufacture and propagation of Zionist propaganda (called *hasbara* in Hebrew) by means of Israel's public education system. No Jewish citizen of Israel escapes this propagandistic "education." Today the *hasbara* process continues not only through the school system but through the government offices of National Public Diplomacy (housed in the prime minister's office), the Ministry of Foreign Affairs, the Israeli Defense Forces, and the Ministry of Diaspora Affairs, as well as through numerous public relations firms, news outlets, and other public media. Throughout the Christian church, Israeli propaganda is passed on to the United States through select dispensational and evangelical Bible colleges, seminaries, churches, Bible retreats, prophecy conferences, bookstores, and films. These Christian sources basically read off the Israeli *hasbara* script and add their own Bible studies to buttress these secular narratives.

15. The cherry tree myth was invented by Washington's biographer, Mason Locke Weems, who first published *The Life of Washington* in 1800; see Richardson, "Cherry Tree Myth."

16. Aderet, "But Sir."

17. Crump, *Like Birds in a Cage*, 50–51.

My goal is not to change pro-Israel people into pro-Palestinian people. My objective, rather, is to help us all become pro-humanity people; to help us all become pro-justice and anti-injustice people; to share the love of God and the grace of Jesus Christ with all people, no matter their ethnicity or the color of their skin. Eventually, I hope that all my readers will understand that political Zionism[18] is incompatible with thoroughgoing Christian discipleship.

The Old Testament prophets continue to challenge us. God still wants his people to lift the downtrodden and to show mercy to the oppressed. By its very nature, political Zionism remains antagonistic to this prophetic vision. When I was a university professor I once had a student who dropped out of the school's ROTC program because he believed that the military values he was being taught in ROTC were diametrically opposed to his maturing understanding of the Christian life.[19] This young man had the spiritual eyes to see that the militaristic propaganda he was being taught day after day was incongruent with his desire to keep in step with the Holy Spirit.

My prayer for you, dear reader, is that you, too, will recognize that neither Jewish nor Christian Zionism will lead you to maturity in the ways of the resurrected Jesus. Instead, follow Jesus by seeking justice for the oppressed. Cry out against genocide in Gaza.[20] Condemn both the Israeli and the US governments for their parts in actively slaughtering innocent Palestinians in Gaza and the West Bank. Call your elected representatives. Sacrifice something of yourself, your time, finances, and energy, in seeking peace and justice in Israel–Palestine. Pray, and then pray some more for God's kingdom to come and God's will to be done in Israel–Palestine as it is done in heaven.

18. Though I haven't delved into the distinctions among the various sorts of Zionism available throughout history, political Zionism is the strain of Jewish supremacy dominant in Israel today. I believe its emphasis on controlling a Jewish ethnocracy in which Palestinians (and others) remain second-class citizens makes it a racist ideology that no Christian of conscience can endorse.

19. You can read his story in Crump, *I Pledge Allegiance*, 148–49.

20. See the compilation of articles in Fisk and Wagner, *Being Christian After the Desolation of Gaza*.

Bibliography

Abraham, Yuval. "'Lavender': The AI Machine Directing Israel's Bombing Spree in Gaza." *+972 Magazine*, Apr. 3, 2024. https://www.972mag.com/lavender-ai-israeli-army-gaza/.

———. "'A Mass Assassination Factory': Inside Israel's Calculated Bombing of Gaza." *+972 Magazine*, Nov. 30, 2023. www.972mag.com/mass-assassination-factory-israel-calculated-bombing-gaza/.

Aderet, Ofer. "'But Sir, It's an American Ship.' 'Never Mind, Hit Her!' When Israel Attacked USS Liberty." *Haaretz*, July 11, 2017. https://www.haaretz.com/us-news/2017-07-11/ty-article/but-sir-its-an-american-ship-never-mind-hit-her/0000017f-e48c-d7b2-a77f-e78f76800000.

Adwan, Sami, et al. "'Victims of Our Own Narratives?' Portrayal of the 'Other' in Israeli and Palestinian School Books." Council of Religious Institutions of the Holy Land, 2013. https://d7hj1xx5r7f3h.cloudfront.net/Israeli-Palestinian_School_Book_Study_Report-English.pdf.

Al Jazeera. "Death Toll from Starvation in Gaza Rises to 115 as Israeli Attacks Continue." July 24, 2025. https://www.aljazeera.com/news/2025/7/24/death-toll-from-starvation-in-gaza-rises-to-115-as-israeli-attacks-continue.

———. "Israeli Defense Minister Orders 'Complete Siege' on Gaza." Oct. 9, 2023. https://www.aljazeera.com/program/newsfeed/2023/10/9/israeli-defence-minister-orders-complete-siege-on-gaza.

al-Orzza, Amaya, and Rachel Hallowell. *Forced Population Transfer: The Case of Palestine, Suppression of Resistance*. Bethlehem: BADIL, 2016.

Amit, Zalman, and Daphna Levit. *Israeli Rejectionism: A Hidden Agenda in the Middle East Peace Process*. London: Pluto, 2011.

Anziska, Seth. *Preventing Palestine: A Political History from Camp David to Oslo*. Princeton: Princeton University Press, 2018.

Aruri, Naseer H. *Dishonest Broker: The U.S. Role in Israel and Palestine*. Cambridge, MA: South End, 2003.

Bayoumi, Moustafa, and Mona Chalabi. "Toys, Spices, Sewing Machines: The Items Israel Banned from Entering Gaza." *The Guardian*, June 24, 2024. https://www.theguardian.com/world/article/2024/jun/24/gaza-blockade-israel-banned-items.

Bell, Daniel M., Jr. *Just War as Christian Discipleship: Recentering the Tradition in the Church Rather Than the State*. Grand Rapids: Brazos, 2009.

Benne, Robert. "Theology and Politics: Reinhold Niebuhr's Christian Zionism." In *The New Christian Zionism: Fresh Perspectives on Israel and the Land*, edited by Gerald R. McDermott, 221–48. Dowers Grove, IL: IVP Academic, 2016.

Blumenthal, Paul. "Israeli President Suggests That Civilians in Gaza Are Legitimate Targets." *HuffPost*, Oct. 16, 2023. https://www.yahoo.com/news/israeli-president-says-no-innocent-154330724.html.

Boxerman, Aaron. "Far-Right Israeli Minister Calls for West Bank to Be Annexed." *New York Times*, Sept. 3, 2025. https://www.nytimes.com/2025/09/03/world/middleeast/israel-west-bank-annexations.html.

Breaking the Silence. "Can No Longer Tell Good from Bad." www.breakingthesilence.org.il/testimonies/database/31766.

———. "Death Sentence for a Man Who Wasn't Armed." www.breakingthesilence.org.il/testimonies/database/100210.

———. "The Kid Got It Bad, for Real." www.breakingthesilence.org.il/testimonies/database/518206.

———. *Military Rule: Testimonies of Soldiers from the Civil Administration, Gaza DCL and COGAT 2011–2021*. Tel Aviv: Breaking the Silence, 2022. https://www.breakingthesilence.org.il/inside/wp-content/uploads/2022/07/Military_rule_testimony_booklet.pdf.

———. "The Organization." https://www.breakingthesilence.org.il/about/organization.

———. *Our Harsh Logic: Israeli Soldiers' Testimonies from the Occupied Territories 2000–2010*. New York: Henry Holt, 2012.

———. "We Smashed Up Everything." www.breakingthesilence.org.il/testimonies/database/70856.

———. "What Is She Going to Become and Who Is She Going to Hate?" www.breakingthesilence.org.il/testimonies/database/802585.

Brody, Shlomo M. *Ethics of Our Fighters: A Jewish View on War and Morality*. Jerusalem: Maggid, 2023.

———. "What Does the Torah Have to Say About Military Ethics?" *Jewish Action*, 2024. jewishaction.com/religion/Jewish-law/what-does-the-torah-have-to-say-about-military-ethics.

Brog, David. *Reclaiming Israel's History: Roots, Rights, and the Struggle for Peace*. Washington, DC: Regnery, 2018.

Bryant, Wes J. "We Must Face the Hard Truth in Gaza: Israel Has Lost Its Moral Authority." *The Hill*, July 18, 2024. https://thehill.com/opinion/international/4777940-idf-gaza-civilian-harm/.

B'Tselem. *Our Genocide*. July 2025. https://www.btselem.org/publications/202507_our_genocide.

———. "Rounds of Fighting in Gaza." https://www.btselem.org/gaza/previous_rounds_of_fighting.

Burge, Gary M. "Christian Zionism as Mythology." Paper presented at the International Consultation on Understanding Christian Zionism and its Effects on Christians in the Middle East, January 23–27, 2025.

———. *Jesus and the Land: The New Testament Challenge to "Holy Land" Theology*. Grand Rapids: Baker Academic, 2010.

Campos, Michelle U. *Ottoman Brothers: Muslims, Christians, and Jews in Early Twentieth-Century Palestine*. Stanford, CA: Stanford University Press, 2011.

Chapman, Colin. *Whose Promised Land? The Continuing Crisis over Israel and Palestine*. Grand Rapids: Baker, 2002.

Chazan, Meir. "The Dispute in Mapai over 'Self-Restraint' and 'Purity of Arms' During the Arab Revolt." *Jewish Social Studies* 15 (Spring/Summer 2009) 89–113.

Central Intelligence Agency. "The Consequences of the Partition of Palestine." Nov. 28, 1947. cia.gov/readingroom/docs/CIA-RDP78-01617A003000180001-8.pdf.

Crump, David M. "Christian Zionist Bible Reading: An Exercise in Unethical Nostalgia." Forthcoming.

———. "Echoes of Slavery, Racial Segregation and Jim Crow: American Dispensationalism and Christian Zionist Bible-Reading." *Journal of Holy Land and Palestine Studies* 23 (2024) 1–17.

———. *I Pledge Allegiance: A Believer's Guide to Kingdom Citizenship in 21st-Century America*. Grand Rapids: Eerdmans, 2018.

———. *Like Birds in a Cage: Christian Zionism's Collusion in Israel's Oppression of the Palestinian People*. Eugene, OR: Cascade, 2021.

Dalrymple, Rob. *Land of Contention: Biblical Narratives and the Struggle for the Holy Land*. Eugene, OR: Cascade, 2024.

———. *These Brothers of Mine: A Biblical Theology of Land and Family and a Response to Christian Zionism*. Eugene, OR: Wipf & Stock, 2015.

Dodd, C. H. *The Epistle of Paul to the Romans*. London: Fontana, 1959.

Douglass, Frederick. *Narrative of the Life of Frederick Douglass, an American Slave*. New York: Union Square, 2022.

Elkins, Caroline. *Legacy of Violence: A History of the British Empire*. New York: Knopf, 2022.

el-Kurd, Mohammed. *Perfect Victims and the Politics of Appeal*. Chicago: Haymarket, 2025.

Ellul, Jacques. *Propaganda: The Formation of Men's Attitudes*. New York: Knopf, 1965.

Erakat, Noura. *Justice for Some: Law and the Question of Palestine*. Stanford, CA: Stanford University Press, 2019.

———. "No, Israel Does Not Have the Right to Self-Defense in International Law Against Occupied Palestinian Territory." *Jadaliyya*, 2012. www.jadaliyya.com/Print/27551.

Euro-Med Human Rights Monitor. "Infographic: 660 Days of Genocide in Gaza." July 29, 2025. https://euromedmonitor.org/en/article/6809/Infographic:-660-days-of-genocide-in-Gaza.

Fabian, Emanuel. "Defense Minister Announces 'Complete Siege' of Gaza: No Power, Food or Fuel." *The Times of Israel*, Oct. 9, 2023. https://www.timesofisrael.com/liveblog_entry/defense-minister-announces-complete-siege-of-gaza-no-power-food-or-fuel/.

Fallon, Peter K. *Propaganda 2.1: Understanding Propaganda in the Digital Age*. Eugene, OR: Cascade, 2022.

Feinberg, John S. "Systems of Discontinuity." In *Continuity and Discontinuity: Perspectives on the Relationship Between the Old and New Testaments: Essays in Honor of S. Lewis Johnson Jr.*, edited by John S. Feinberg, 63–86. Westchester, IL: Crossway, 1988.

Feinberg, Paul D. "Hermeneutics of Discontinuity." In *Continuity and Discontinuity: Perspectives on the Relationship Between the Old and New Testaments: Essays in Honor of S. Lewis Johnson Jr.*, edited by John S. Feinberg, 109–28. Westchester, IL: Crossway, 1988.

Ferguson, Niall. "Hamas 'Intending Nothing Less Than a Second Holocaust.'" *The Australian*, Dec. 6, 2023. https://web.archive.org/web/20240311111155/https://www.theaustralian.com.au/commentary/hamas-intending-nothing-less-than-a-second-holocaust-niall-ferguson/video/248ab4e66a7ed0b5ac3180537e065024.

Finkelstein, Norman G. *Method and Madness: The Hidden Story of Israel's Assaults on Gaza*. New York: OR Books, 2014.

Fisk, Bruce N. "Genesis 12:3, Christian Zionism, and Blessing Israel." *Bibliotheca Sacra* 180 (Apr.–June 2023) 144–63.

Fisk, Bruce N., and J. Ross Wagner, eds. *Being Christian After the Desolation of Gaza*. Eugene, OR: Cascade, 2025.

Flapan, Simha. *The Birth of Israel: Myths and Realities*. New York: Pantheon, 1987.

———. *Zionism and the Palestinians*. London: Croom Helm, 1979.

Geneva Conventions of 1949. *Convention (I) for the Amelioration of the Condition of the Wounded and Sick in Armed Forces in the Field*. Geneva, Aug. 12, 1949. https://ihl-databases.icrc.org/en/ihl-treaties/gci-1949?activeTab=1949GCs-APs-and-commentaries.

———. *Convention (IV) Relative to the Protection of Civilian Persons in Time of War*. Geneva, Aug. 12, 1949. https://ihl-databases.icrc.org/en/ihl-treaties/gciv-1949?activeTab=1949GCs-APs-and-commentaries.

Gerges, Fawaz A. "Egypt and the 1948 War: Internal Conflict and Regional Ambition." In *The War for Palestine*, edited by Eugene L. Rogan and Avi Shlaim, 150–75. New York: Cambridge University Press, 2007.

Glubb, John. *Soldier with the Arabs*. London: Hodder and Stoughton, 1957.

Goldenberg, Tia. "Harsh Israeli Rhetoric Against Palestinians Becomes Central to South Africa's Genocide Case." AP, Jan. 18, 2024. https://apnews.com/article/israel-palestinians-south-africa-genocide-hate-speech-97a9e4a84a3a6bebeddfb80f8a030724.

The Hague Conventions. "Convention (II) with Respect to the Laws and Customs of War on Land and Its Annex: Regulations Concerning the Laws and Customs of War on Land." The Hague, July 29, 1899. https://ihl-databases.icrc.org/en/ihl-treaties/hague-conv-ii-1899?activeTab=.

Haidar, Dalia. "'Wounded Child, No Surviving Family': The Pain of Gaza's Orphans." *BBC News*, Dec. 4, 2023. https://www.bbc.com/news/world-middle-east-67614139.

Hajjar, Lisa. "Is Gaza Still Occupied and Why Does It Matter?" *Jadaliyya*, 2012. https://www.jadaliyya.com/Details/27557.

———. "Israel as Innovator in the Attempted Mainstreaming of Extreme Violence." *Middle East Report* no. 279 (Summer 2016) 38–45.

Halper, Jeff. "How Israel Undermines International Law Through 'Lawfare.'" ICAHD, Aug. 18, 2014. icahd.org/2019/05/24/how-israel-undermines-international-law-through-lawfare/.

Hasson, Nir, and Chen Maanit. "A Lost Battle for Human Rights: Throughout the War Israel's High Court Has Denied All Requests to Protect Gazans." *Haaretz*, May 23, 2025. https://www.haaretz.com/magazine/2025-05-23/ty-article-magazine/.premium/throughout-the-war-israels-high-court-denied-requests-to-protect-gazans-human-rights/00000196-f8ac-d7c4-a9b6-fcae72440000.

Herman, Edward S., and Noam Chomsky. *Manufacturing Consent: The Political Economy of the Mass Media*. New York: Pantheon, 2002.

Herzl, Theodor. *The Jewish State*. N.p.: 2014.

Hoffman, Joshua. "The Jewish Commandments of War." *Future of Jewish*, Oct. 6, 2024. www.futureofjewish.com/p/judaisms-codes-of-war.

Horner, Barry E. *Future Israel: Why Christian Anti-Judaism Must Be Challenged.* Nashville: B&H Academic, 2007.

Hughes, Matthew. "Collusion Across the Litani? Lebanon and the 1948 War." In *The War for Palestine*, edited by Eugene L. Rogan and Avi Shlaim, 204–27. Cambridge: Cambridge University Press, 2007.

———. "Terror in Galilee: British–Jewish Collaboration and the Special Night Squads in Palestine During the Arab Revolt, 1938–39." *Journal of Imperial and Commonwealth History* 43 (2015) 590–610.

Hummel, Daniel G. "The Bestselling Reference Bible That Remade American Evangelicalism." Text and Canon Institute, July 1, 2024. https://textandcanon.org/the-bestselling-reference-bible-that-remade-american-evangelicalism/.

———. *Covenant Brothers: Evangelicals, Jews, and U.S.–Israeli Relations.* Philadelphia: University of Pennsylvania Press, 2019.

Institute for Middle East Understanding. "Explainer: The Dahiya Doctrine and Israel's Use of Disproportionate Force." July 31, 2024. imeu.org/article/the-dahiya-doctrine-and-israels-use-of-disproportionate-force.

International Court of Justice. "Application of the Convention on the Prevention and Punishment of the Crime of Genocide in the Gaza Strip (South Africa *v.* Israel)." Dec. 29, 2023. https://icj-cij.org/sites/default/files/case-related/192/192-20231228-app-01-00-en.pdf.

Israel Defense Forces. "Our Mission and Our Values." https://www.idf.il/en/mini-sites/our-mission-our-values/.

Jacobson, Abigail, and Moshe Naor. *Oriental Neighbors: Middle Eastern Jews and Arabs in Mandatory Palestine.* Waltham, MA: Brandeis University Press, 2016.

Jewish Virtual Library. "Israel Defense Forces: Ruach Tzahal—Code of Ethics." https://www.jewishvirtuallibrary.org/ruach-tzahal-idf-code-of-ethics.

Jones, Owen. "Israel Has Deliberately Starved the People of Gaza. It Couldn't Have Done It Without the West's Help." *The Guardian*, July 30, 2025. https://www.theguardian.com/commentisfree/2025/jul/30/israel-starvation-gaza-keir-starmer-west.

Karsh, Efraim. *Palestine Betrayed.* New Haven: Yale University Press, 2010.

Khalidi, Muhammad Ali. "'The Most Moral Army in the World': The New 'Ethical Code' of the Israeli Military and the War on Gaza." *Journal of Palestine Studies* 39 (Spring 2010) 6–23.

Khalidi, Rashid. *Brokers of Deceit: How the US Has Undermined Peace in the Middle East.* Boston: Beacon, 2013.

Khalidi, Walid, ed. *All That Remains: The Palestinian Villages Occupied and Depopulated by Israel in 1948.* Washington, DC: Institute for Palestine Studies, 1992.

Kingsley, Patrick, et al. "Israel Loosened Its Rules to Bomb Hamas Fighters, Killing Many More Civilians." *New York Times*, Dec. 26, 2024. https://www.nytimes.com/2024/12/26/world/middleeast/israel-hamas-gaza-bombing.html.

Knesset. Basic Law: Israel as the Nation-State of the Jewish People. https://main.knesset.gov.il/EN/activity/documents/BasicLawsPDF/BasicLawNationState.pdf.

Kornbluh, Jacob. "He Was the Head of Christians United for Israel. Now He's Running as a Jewish Candidate for Congress." *Forward*, May 8, 2022. https://forward.com/news/501610/david-brog-nevada-election-christians-united-for-israel-congress/.

Kuttler, Hillel. "75 Years After His Death, Why Orde Wingate Remains a Hero in Israel." *Times of Israel*, Mar. 23, 2019. https://www.timesofisrael.com/75-years-after-his-death-why-orde-wingate-remains-a-hero-in-israel/.

Landis, Joshua. "Syria and the Palestine War: Fighting King 'Abdullah's 'Greater Syria Plan.'" In *The War for Palestine*, edited by Eugene L. Rogan and Avi Shlaim, 176–203. New York: Cambridge University Press, 2007.

Larsen, David L. *Jews, Gentiles and the Church: A New Perspective on History and Prophecy*. Grand Rapids: Discovery House, 1995.

Lewis, Bernard. *End of Modern History in the Middle East*. Stanford, CA: Hoover Institution, 2011.

———. *The Jews of Islam*. Princeton: Princeton University Press, 2014.

———. *Semites and Anti-Semites: An Inquiry into Conflict and Prejudice*. New York: Norton, 1999.

Lewis, Donald. *The Origins of Christian Zionism: Lord Shaftesbury and Evangelical Support for a Jewish Homeland*. Cambridge: Cambridge University Press, 2010.

Lewis, Larry. "Israeli Civilian Harm Mitigation in Gaza: Gold Standard or Fool's Gold?" *Just Security*, Mar. 12, 2024. https://www.justsecurity.org/93105/israeli-civilian-harm-mitigation-in-gaza-gold-standard-or-fools-gold/.

Levy, Gideon. *The Killing of Gaza: Reports on a Catastrophe*. London: Verso, 2024.

Lindsey, Hal. *The Everlasting Hatred: The Roots of Jihad*. Washington, DC: WND Books, 2011.

Louis, Wm. Roger, and Avi Shlaim, eds. *The 1967 Arab–Israeli War: Origins and Consequences*. Cambridge: Cambridge University Press, 2018.

MacPherson, Myra. All *Governments Lie! The Life and Times of Rebel Journalist I. F. Stone*. New York: Scribner, 2006.

Makdisi, Ussama. *Age of Coexistence: The Ecumenical Frame and the Making of the Modern Arab World*. Oakland: University of California Press, 2019.

Marei, Fouad Gehad. "Dahiya Doctrine." In *Conflict in the Modern Middle East: An Encyclopedia of Civil War, Revolutions and Regime Change*, edited by Jonathan K. Zartman, 75–76. Santa Barbara, CA: ABC-CLIO, 2020.

May, Rollo. *The Cry for Myth*. New York: Norton, 1991.

McKernan, Bethan, and Harry Davies. "'The Machine Did It Coldly': Israel Used AI to Identify 37,000 Hamas Targets." *The Guardian*, Apr. 3, 2024. www.theguardian.com/world/2024/apr/03/israel-gaza-ai-database-hamas-airstrikes.

Merom, Gil. "Israel's National Security and the Myth of Exceptionalism." *Political Science Quarterly* 114 (Autumn 1999) 409–34.

Middle East Monitor. "Israel MK Calls for a Second Nakba in Gaza." Oct. 9, 2023. https://www.middleeastmonitor.com/20231009-israel-mk-calls-for-a-second-nakba-in-gaza/.

Moore, Russell. "American Christians Should Stand with Israel Under Attack." *Christianity Today*, Oct. 7, 2023. https://www.christianitytoday.com/2023/10/israel-hamas-middle-east-war-christians/.

Morris, Benny. *1948 and After: Israel and the Palestinians*. Oxford: Clarendon, 1994.

———. *1948: The First Arab–Israeli War*. New Haven: Yale University Press, 2008.

———. *The Birth of the Palestinian Refugee Problem Revisited*. Cambridge: Cambridge University Press, 2004.

———. "The New Historiography: Israel and Its Past." Chap. 1 in *1948 and After: Israel and the Palestinians*. Oxford: Clarendon, 1994.

———. *Righteous Victims: A History of the Zionist–Arab Conflict, 1881–2001*. New York: Vintage, 2001.

NBC News. "American Survivor of Israeli Music Festival Attack 'Happy to Be Alive.'" YouTube video, Oct. 20, 2023. https://www.youtube.com/watch?v=CBLcfh82NbE.

Netanyahu, Benjamin. "Statement by PM Netanyahu." Ministry of Foreign Affairs, Oct. 18, 2023. https://www.gov.il/en/pages/pm-netanyahu-statement-18-oct-2023.

———. "Statement by PM Netanyahu." The Prime Minister's Office, Oct. 28, 2023. https://www.gov.il/en/pages/event-statement281023.

Nowlin, Sanford. "Apocalypse Now: Why Pastor John Hagee Has Never Been More Politically Powerful—and Terrifying." *San Antonio Current*, Sept. 19, 2019. https://www.sacurrent.com/the-daily/archives/2019/09/10/apocalypse-now-why-pastor-john-hagee-has-never-been-more-politically-powerful-or-terrifying.

NowThis Impact. "Hypocritical Media Coverage of Ukraine vs. the Middle East." YouTube video, Mar. 1, 2022. https://www.youtube.com/watch?v=2z9UyPurVok.

OCHA. "Considerations for the Delivery of Humanitarian Aid During a Cease Fire in Gaza." United Nations. https://www.unocha.org/considerations-delivery-humanitarian-aid-during-ceasefire-gaza.

O'Malley, Padraig. *The Two-State Delusion: Israel and Palestine—A Tale of Two Narratives*. New York: Viking, 2015.

Orr, Akiva. *The unJewish State: The Politics of Jewish Identity in Israel*. London: Ithaca, 1983.

Pacchiani, Gianluca. "COGAT Chief Addresses Gazans: 'You Wanted Hell, You Will Get Hell.'" *Times of Israel*, Oct. 10, 2023. https://www.timesofisrael.com/liveblog_entry/cogat-chief-addresses-gazans-you-wanted-hell-you-will-get-hell/.

Palumbo, Michael. *The Palestinian Catastrophe: The 1948 Expulsion of a People from Their Homeland*. London: Faber & Faber, 1987.

Pappé, Ilan. *The Ethnic Cleansing of Palestine*. Oxford: Oneworld, 2006.

———. *Lobbying for Zionism on Both Sides of the Atlantic*. London: Oneworld, 2024.

———. *The Making of the Arab–Israeli Conflict 1947–1951*. London: I. B. Tauris, 1992.

———. *Ten Myths About Israel*. London: Verso, 2017.

———. *A Very Short History of the Israel–Palestine Conflict*. London: OneWorld, 2024.

Patterson, Eric. *A Basic Guide to the Just War Tradition: Christian Foundations and Practices*. Grand Rapids: Baker Academic, 2023.

Peled-Elhanan, Nurit. *Holocaust Education and the Semiotics of Othering in Israeli Schoolbooks: The Representation of Holocaust Victims, Jewish "Ethnicities" and Arab "Minorities" in Israeli Schoolbooks*. Champaign, IL: Common Ground Research Networks, 2023.

———. *Palestine in Israeli School Books: Ideology and Propaganda in Education*. London: I. B. Tauris, 2012.

Peters, Joan. *From Time Immemorial: The Origins of the Arab–Jewish Conflict over Palestine*. New York: Harper & Row, 1984.

Quigley, John. *The Case for Palestine: An International Law Perspective*. Durham, NC: Duke University Press, 2005.

Rapaport, Nadav. "Nearly Half of Israelis Support Army Killing All Palestinians in Gaza, Poll Finds." *Middle East Eye*, May 24, 2025. https://www.middleeasteye.net/news/majority-israelis-support-expulsion-palestinians-gaza-poll.

Reuters. "Israel Warns Hizbullah War Would Invite Destruction." YNet Global, Oct. 3, 2008. https://www.ynetnews.com/articles/0,7340,L-3604893,00.html.

Richardson, Jay. "Cherry Tree Myth." George Washington's Mt. Vernon, Oct. 4, 2023. https://www.mountvernon.org/library/digitalhistory/digital-encyclopedia/article/cherry-tree-myth.

Robinson, Shira. *Citizen Strangers: Palestinians and the Birth of Israel's Liberal Settler State*. Stanford, CA: Stanford University Press, 2013.

Rogan, Eugene L. "Jordan and 1948: The Persistence of an Official History." In *The War for Palestine*, edited by Eugene L. Rogan and Avi Shlaim, 104–24. New York: Cambridge University Press, 2007.

Rogan, Eugene L., and Avi Shlaim, eds. *The War for Palestine*. New York: Cambridge University Press, 2007.

Rouhana, Nadim N., and Sahar S. Huneidi, eds. *Israel and Its Palestinian Citizens: Ethnic Privileges in the Jewish State*. Cambridge: Cambridge University Press, 2017.

Rydelnik, Michael. "The Hermeneutics of the Conflict." In *Israel, the Church and the Middle East*, edited by Darrell Bock and Mitch Glaser, 63–82. Grand Rapids: Kregel, 2018.

Said, Edward W. *Covering Islam: How the Media and the Experts Determine How We See the Rest of the World*. New York: Vintage, 1997.

———. *Orientalism*. New York: Vintage, 1979.

———. *The Question of Palestine*. New York: Vintage, 1992.

Scofield, C. I., ed. *The Scofield Reference Bible*. New York: Oxford University Press, 1917.

———. *The New Scofield Reference Bible*. Edited by E. Schuyler English et al. New York: Oxford University Press, 1967.

Shaw, Martin. "The Uses and Abuses of the Term 'Genocide' in Gaza." *New Lines Magazine*, Nov. 6, 2023. https://web.archive.org/web/20240301125252/https://newlinesmag.com/spotlight/the-uses-and-abuses-of-the-term-genocide-in-gaza/.

Shlaim, Avi. *Collusion Across the Jordan: King Abdullah, the Zionist Movement, and the Partition of Palestine*. New York: Columbia University Press, 1988.

———. "The Debate About 1948." *International Journal of Middle East Studies* 27 (Aug. 1995) 287–304.

———. *Genocide in Gaza: Israel's Long War on Palestine*. Belfast: Irish Pages, 2024.

———. *The Iron Wall: Israel and the Arab World*. New York: Norton, 2001.

———. "Israel and the Arab Coalition in 1948." In *The War for Palestine*, edited by Eugene L. Rogan and Avi Shlaim, 79–103. New York: Cambridge University Press, 2007.

———. *The Politics of Partition: King Abdullah, the Zionists, and Palestine 1921–1951*. Oxford: Oxford University Press, 1998.

———. "Ten Years After the First War on Gaza, Israel Still Plans Endless Brute Force." *The Guardian*, Jan. 7, 2019. https://www.theguardian.com/commentisfree/2019/jan/07/ten-years-first-war-gaza-operation-cast-lead-israel-brute-force.

———. *Three Worlds: Memoirs of an Arab-Jew*. London: Oneworld, 2023.

Shupak, Greg. *The Wrong Story: Palestine, Israel, and the Media*. New York: OR Books, 2018.

Shurafa, Wafaa, and Samy Magdy. "Over 60,000 Have Died in the Israel–Hamas War, Gaza's Health Ministry Says." *PBS News*, July 29, 2025. https://www.pbs.org/newshour/world/over-60000-palestinians-have-died-in-the-israel-hamas-war-gazas-health-ministry-says.

Silver, Laura, and Maria Smerkovich. "Israeli Views of the Israel–Hamas War." Pew Research Center, May 30, 2024. pewresearch.org/global/2024/05/30/israeli-views-of-the-israel-hamas-war/.

Spagat, Mike. "Netanyahu Got It Wrong Before the US Congress: IDF's Clean Performance in Gaza Is a Lie." *Action on Armed Violence*, Aug. 2, 2024. https://aoav.org.uk/2024/netanyahu-got-it-wrong-before-the-us-congress-idfs-clean-performance-in-gaza-is-a-lie/.

Spector, Stephen. *Evangelicals and Israel: The Story of American Christian Zionism*. Oxford: Oxford University Press, 2009.

Spencer, John. "Israel Implemented More Measures to Prevent Civilian Casualties Than Any Other Nation in History." *Newsweek*, Jan. 31, 2024. www.newsweek.com/israel-implemented-more-measures-prevent-civilian-casualties-any-other-nation-history-opinion-1865613.

Stern, Marilyn. "John Spencer on Israel's Urban War in Gaza: A Technical Analysis." Middle East Forum, Jan. 24, 2025. www.meforum.org/podcasts/john-spencer-on-israels-urban-war-in-gaza-a-technical-analysis.

Strenski, Ivan. *Four Theories of Myth in Twentieth-Century History: Cassirer, Eliade, Lévi-Strauss and Malinowski*. Iowa City: University of Iowa Press, 1987.

Suarez, Thomas. *State of Terror: How Terrorism Created Modern Israel*. North Hampton, MA: Olive Branch, 2017.

Swisher, Clayton E. *The Palestine Papers: The End of the Road?* Chatham, UK: Hesperus, 2011.

———. *The Truth About Camp David: The Untold Story About the Collapse of the Middle East Peace Process*. New York: Nation Books, 2004.

Taylor, Adam. "With Strikes Targeting Rockets and Tunnels, the Israeli Tactic of 'Mowing the Grass' Returns to Gaza." *Washington Post*, May 14, 2021. https://www.washingtonpost.com/world/2021/05/14/israel-gaza-history/.

Tripp, Charles. "Iraq and the 1948 War: Mirror of Iraq's Disorder." In *The War for Palestine*, edited by Eugene L. Rogan and Avi Shlaim, 125–49. New York: Cambridge University Press, 2007.

Turfah, Mary. "The Most Moral Army." *Los Angeles Review of Books*, Oct. 1, 2024. https://lareviewofbooks.org/article/the-most-moral-army/.

United Nations. *The Legality of the Israeli Occupation*. New York: United Nations, 2023. https://digitallibrary.un.org/record/4025075?ln=en&v=pdf.

United Nations General Assembly. "Declaration on Principles of International Law Concerning Friendly Relations and Cooperation Among States in Accordance with the Charter of the United Nations." 1970. https://digitallibrary.un.org/record/202170?ln=en&v=pdf.

———. "The Question of Palestine." 1974. https://www.un.org/unispal/wp-content/uploads/2016/05/ARES3236XXIX.pdf.

———. "Right of the Palestinian People to Self-Determination." Resolution 34/29. Mar. 24, 2017. https://docs.un.org/en/a/hrc/res/34/29.

———. "The Situation in the Middle East." Resolution 32/20. 1977. https://digitallibrary.un.org/record/187833?ln=en&v=pdf.

United Nations Security Council. "Resolution 242 (1967)." Nov. 22, 1967. https://digitallibrary.un.org/record/90717?v=pdf.

———. "Resolution 2334 (2016)." Dec. 23, 2016. https://digitallibrary.un.org/record/853446?ln=en&v=pdf.

Vlach, Michael J. *Has the Church Replaced Israel? A Theological Evaluation*. Nashville: B&H Academic, 2010.

Wikipedia. "Animal Stereotypes of Palestinians in Israeli Discourse." https://en.wikipedia.org/wiki/animal_stereotypes_of_Palestinians_in_Israeli_discourse.

———. "Dispensationalism." https://en.wikipedia.org/wiki/Dispensationalism.

Wilde, Ralph. "The International Law of Self-Determination and the Use of Force Requires an Immediate End to the Occupation of the Palestinian West Bank and Gaza." University College London Policy Brief, July 2022. https://www.ucl.ac.uk/laws/sites/laws/files/2025-09/ralph_wilde_palestine_policy_brief.pdf.

———. "Israel's War in Gaza Is Not a Valid Act of Self-Defence in International Law." *Opinio Juris*, Nov. 9, 2023. https://opiniojuris.org/2023/11/09/israels-war-in-gaza-is-not-a-valid-act-of-self-defence-in-international-law/.

———. "Is the Israeli Occupation of the Palestinian West Bank (Including East Jerusalem) and Gaza 'Legal' or 'Illegal' Under International Law?" University College London, Nov. 29, 2022. bit.ly/ralph-wilde-oPt.

Wilkins, Brett. "Netanyahu Accused of 'Genocidal Intentions' in Gaza After 'Holy Mission' Speech." *Common Dreams*, Oct. 30, 2023. commondreams.org/news/netanyahu-genocide.

———. "'We Are Too Humane. Burn Gaza Now,' Says Senior Israeli Lawmaker." *Common Dreams*, Nov. 18, 2023. https://www.commondreams.org/news/gaza-genocide.

Yacovone, Donald. *Teaching White Supremacy: America's Democratic Ordeal and the Forging of Our National Identity*. New York: Pantheon, 2022.

Yiftachel, Oren. *Ethnocracy: Land and Identity Politics in Israel/Palestine*. Philadelphia: University of Pennsylvania Press, 2006.

Zion, Noam. "Purity of Arms: Educating Ethical Warriors in the Israeli Army." Jerusalem: Shalom Hartman Institute, 2016. shi-webfiles.s3.amazonaws.com/Study_Noam_Zion_2016_Purity_of_Arms_Curriculum.pdf.

SUBJECT INDEX

SCRIPTURE INDEX

2 Corinthians

Galatians

Ephesians

1 Thessalonians

2 Thessalonians

1 Peter

Revelation

www.ingramcontent.com/pod-product-compliance
Lightning Source LLC
LaVergne TN
LVHW090524110826
845146LV00003B/967

* 9 7 9 8 3 8 5 2 4 3 0 5 1 *